Annual Editions:
Economics,
Thirty-Eighth Edition

Sudip Ghosh

http://create.mheducation.com

ISBN-10: 1259176940   ISBN-13: 9781259176944

Contents

Unit 5 93

Unit 6 113

Preface

Economics, once dubbed as "dismal science," is no longer true since the Global Recession unfolded. Millions of jobs were lost mostly in industrialized nations and assets worth trillions of dollars were destroyed. Bold actions by U.S. policy makers in coalescence with their G20 partners helped in the recovery effort and the turnaround was quick but modest. Amid all these, key economic events unfolded in the U.S. since 2013 which has global ramifications.

The objective of the 38th edition is to provide a wide range of articles in economics from the introduction of the health care bill, illegal immigration, legalization of medical and recreational marijuana, raising minimum wage, gender equality, unemployment, not to forget the inception of bitcoins, crowdfunding, etc. Since interests in economics have recently been renewed, our hope is to provide interesting articles and generate curiosity among young readers.

First, the Affordable Care Act (ACA) (popularly known as "Obamacare") was implemented primarily to contain healthcare costs. From the very onset ACA has been a source of controversy with supporters and opponents disagreeing on everything from reduced premiums, affordability, and eligibility of coverage. Second, the U.S. recovery has been promising; the labor force participation rate at 62.8 percent is at its lowest questioning the efficacy of monetary policy of "quantitative easing" (QE) initiated by the Fed to jumpstart the economy. Third, the financial crisis various regulations were put in place to protect U.S. investors and taxpayers alike. Thus far the process has worked, from early 2009 when the S & P 500 index bottomed at 700, the broad stock market average has more than tripled by artificially keeping interest rates low and over valuing equities. Fourth, the U.S. has an unemployment rate of 6.3 percent; yet, we constantly hear from employers that they can't fill positions, particularly those that require higher skills. There is a clear disconnect between vocation and education. The government is addressing the issue by creating an initiative to work with community colleges, vocational tech schools, and local businesses to align education and training to fill in skill-based better paying jobs. Another related topic is about raising minimum U.S. millions of Americans who work hard in jobs that pay too little and offer too few benefits. However, raising the federal minimum wage (to $10.10 an hour) would benefit about 25 million workers, lift 5 million to 6 million people out of poverty, strengthen our economy, and save taxpayers billions of dollars in handouts. Fifth, the presence of undocumented workers and how to integrate them as legal work force has been particularly challenging. Sixth, legalization of medical marijuana in 23 states is quite significant. Several economists pointed out that legalizing pot will help jumpstart the economy to the tune of $100 billion a year or more instead of costing the U.S. taxpayers $13.7 billion per year in terms of incarceration and other related costs. Seventh, the genesis of bitcoins, crowdfunding, etc., where individuals use computer platform to transact and raise capital is still new; nonetheless, monitoring and compliance from such transactions has been very tricky.

The international arena has been not been quiet either. Amid tepid U.S. recovery, the global economy remains weak due to Chinese economic slowdown coupled with geopolitical uncertainty in the Middle East, Ukraine, Nigeria, etc. It is quite disconcerting to see emerging economies experiencing double digit inflation and high unemployment rate thus threatening global growth. Moreover, greenhouse gas, global warming, and carbon emission are changing the weather pattern and impacting human lives in unimaginable ways. Despite all these, billions of people are striving to better their lives by demanding goods and services from the global market place using Internet and other available technologies.

To summarize, we maintain that for a global economic turnaround, both the U.S. and Chinese economy should continue on the path of recovery and bring emerging markets and the Euro area on board. On the policy side, a concerted global central banking policy which is more transparent should be adopted. G20 countries need to exercise fiscal discipline to avoid austerity measures which is impacting the Euro area in a dramatic way and hindering growth. Given this backdrop, it is essential to bring in the most up-to-date material for our prospective readers where they can connect economic theory with practice.

Sudip Ghosh
Editor

Academic Advisory Board

Members of the Academic Advisory Board are instrumental in the final selection of articles for Annual Editions books and Express Books. Their review of the articles for content, level, and appropriateness provides critical direction to the editor(s) and staff. We think that you will find their careful consideration reflected here.

David Cullipher
Arkansas State University

Dennis Debrecht
Carroll University

Hardial Dulay
Butte College

Arlene Geiger
John Jay College—CUNY

John Nader
Davenport University/Grace Bible College

Anthony Negbenebor
Gardner-Webb University

Marianne Partee
SUNY Erie Community College

Pearl Steinbuch
Mount Ida College

TaMika Steward
Tarrant County College SE

Paul A. Stock
University Of Mary Hardin-Baylor

Correlation Guide

The *Annual Editions* series provides students with convenient, inexpensive access to current, carefully selected articles from the public press. **Annual Editions: Economics, 38/e** is an easy-to-use reader that presents articles on important topics such as *microeconomics and macroeconomics, the bitcoin, off shoring, the global economy,* and many more. For more information on Annual Editions and other McGraw-Hill Create™ titles and collections, visit www.mcgrawhillcreate.com.

This convenient guide matches the units in **Annual Editions: Economics, 38/e** with the corresponding chapters **Economics, 20/e by McConnell et al.**

Economics, 20/e By McConnell et al.	Annual Editions: Economics, 38/e
Chapter 1: Limits, Alternatives, and Choices	Austerity on the Side: EU Hits Restaurateurs with Olive Oil Law Bitcoin Only Worth What People Think It Is Worth Can Medicare Costs Be Tamed? Crowdfunding Diplomacy: the Next Frontier for Government Economic Shocks Reverberate in World of Interconnected Trade Ties Gender Pay and Leadership Gaps Are Real—and Impact Our Economy There's a Fly in My Soup: Can Insects Satisfy World Food Needs? The Effect of Immigrants on U.S. Employment and Productivity
Chapter 2: The Market System and the Circular Flow	13 States Raising Pay for Minimum-Wage Workers Can Better Regulation Boost Growth? Can Medicare Costs Be Tamed? Economic Shocks Reverberate in World of Interconnected Trade Ties Economy Will Benefit from Immigration Reform Gender Pay and Leadership Gaps Are Real—and Impact Our Economy Panic Over US Tapering, China Growth Overdone, Insists IIF Reaching Out to Dropouts Should China Worry About a GDP Slowdown? Who Lives Longest?—Healthy, Wealthy—and Famous
Chapter 3: Demand, Supply, and Market Equilibrium	13 States Raising Pay for Minimum-Wage Workers Bitcoin Only Worth What People Think It Is Worth Can Medicare Costs Be Tamed? Crowdfunding Diplomacy: the Next Frontier for Government Gender Pay and Leadership Gaps Are Real—and Impact Our Economy Immigration Reform Could Boost U.S. Economy Interest in Pot Revenue at New High Price Tag for Childhood Obesity: $19,000 Per Kid Why Colorado and Washington Were Wise to Legalize Pot
Chapter 4: Market Failures: Public Goods and Externalities	13 States Raising Pay for Minimum-Wage Workers Bitcoin Only Worth What People Think It Is Worth Can Medicare Costs Be Tamed? Crowdfunding Diplomacy: the Next Frontier for Government Gender Pay and Leadership Gaps Are Real—and Impact Our Economy Interest in Pot Revenue at New High Price Tag for Childhood Obesity: $19,000 Per Kid Why Colorado and Washington Were Wise to Legalize Pot RPT-Obamacare Is on the Horizon, but Will Enough People Sign Up?
Chapter 5: Government's Role and Government Failure	13 States Raising Pay for Minimum-Wage Workers Can Better Regulation Boost Growth? Can Medicare Costs Be Tamed? Economic Shocks Reverberate in World of Interconnected Trade Ties Economy Will Benefit from Immigration Reform Freezing Paradise: an Update on Global Gender Equality Gender Pay and Leadership Gaps Are Real—and Impact Our Economy Immigration Reform Could Boost U.S. Economy Is 'Amnesty' a Possibility Now? Price Tag for Childhood Obesity: $19,000 Per Kid Reaching Out to Dropouts RPT-Obamacare Is on the Horizon, but Will Enough People Sign Up? Unemployment Rate

Economics, 20/e By McConnell et al.	Annual Editions: Economics, 38/e
Chapter 6: Elasticity	13 States Raising Pay for Minimum-Wage Workers After $75,000, Money Can't Buy Day-to-Day Happiness Can Better Regulation Boost Growth? Can Medicare Costs Be Tamed? Immigration and Happiness Immigration Reform Could Boost U.S. Economy Interest in Pot Revenue at New High Price Tag for Childhood Obesity: $19,000 Per Kid Virtual Health Care Gaining Ground Who Lives Longest?—Healthy, Wealthy—and Famous
Chapter 7: Utility Maximization	13 States Raising Pay for Minimum-Wage Workers Can Better Regulation Boost Growth? Can Medicare Costs Be Tamed? Economy Will Benefit from Immigration Reform Freezing Paradise: an Update on Global Gender Equality Gender Pay and Leadership Gaps Are Real—and Impact Our Economy Price Tag for Childhood Obesity: $19,000 Per Kid Reaching Out to Dropouts Who Lives Longest?—Healthy, Wealthy—and Famous Immigration and Happiness
Chapter 8: Behavioral Economics	13 States Raising Pay for Minimum-Wage Workers Bitcoin Only Worth What People Think It Is Worth Can Better Regulation Boost Growth? Crowdfunding Diplomacy: the Next Frontier for Government Freezing Paradise: an Update on Global Gender Equality Gender Pay and Leadership Gaps Are Real—and Impact Our Economy Immigration Reform Could Boost U.S. Economy Interest in Pot Revenue at New High New Study Suggests eBooks Could Negatively Affect How We Comprehend What We Read Panic Over US Tapering, China Growth Overdone, Insists IIF Price Tag for Childhood Obesity: $19,000 Per Kid There's a Fly in My Soup: Can Insects Satisfy World Food Needs?
Chapter 9: Businesses and the Cost of Production	13 States Raising Pay for Minimum-Wage Workers Can Better Regulation Boost Growth? Freezing Paradise: an Update on Global Gender Equality Gender Pay and Leadership Gaps Are Real—and Impact Our Economy Is 'Amnesty' a Possibility Now? Reaching Out to Dropouts Weakly Capitalized Banks Slowed Lending Recovery After Recession
Chapter 10: Pure Competition in the Short Run	13 States Raising Pay for Minimum-Wage Workers Austerity on the Side: EU Hits Restaurateurs with Olive Oil Law Economic Shocks Reverberate in World of Interconnected Trade Ties Interest in Pot Revenue at New High There's a Fly in My Soup: Can Insects Satisfy World Food Needs? Why Colorado and Washington Were Wise to Legalize Pot
Chapter 11: Pure Competition in the Long Run	13 States Raising Pay for Minimum-Wage Workers After $75,000, Money Can't Buy Day-to-Day Happiness Bitcoin Only Worth What People Think It Is Worth Bitcoin: Why Businesses are Buying in, Despite Critics and Start-Up Woes Crowdfunding Diplomacy: the Next Frontier for Government Interest in Pot Revenue at New High RPT-Obamacare Is on the Horizon, but Will Enough People Sign Up? Virtual Health Care Gaining Ground Why Colorado and Washington Were Wise to Legalize Pot

Economics, 20/e By McConnell et al.	Annual Editions: Economics, 38/e
Chapter 12: Pure Monopoly	After $75,000, Money Can't Buy Day-to-Day Happiness
Chapter 13: Monopolistic Competition and Oligopoly	Crowdfunding Diplomacy: the Next Frontier for Government Interest in Pot Revenue at New High RPT-Obamacare Is on the Horizon, but Will Enough People Sign Up? Virtual Health Care Gaining Ground
Chapter 14: The Demand for Resources	Bitcoin: Why Businesses are Buying in, Despite Critics and Start-Up Woes Can Medicare Costs Be Tamed? Crowdfunding Diplomacy: the Next Frontier for Government Economic Shocks Reverberate in World of Interconnected Trade Ties Interest in Pot Revenue at New High The Effect of Immigrants on U.S. Employment and Productivity Virtual Health Care Gaining Ground Why Colorado and Washington Were Wise to Legalize Pot
Chapter 15: Wage Determination	Who Lives Longest?—Healthy, Wealthy—and Famous
Chapter 16: Rent, Interest, and Profit	13 States Raising Pay for Minimum-Wage Workers Interest in Pot Revenue at New High The Effect of Immigrants on U.S. Employment and Productivity Virtual Health Care Gaining Ground Weakly Capitalized Banks Slowed Lending Recovery After Recession Why Colorado and Washington Were Wise to Legalize Pot
Chapter 17: Natural Resource and Energy Economics	Austerity on the Side: EU Hits Restaurateurs with Olive Oil Law Interest in Pot Revenue at New High The Effect of Immigrants on U.S. Employment and Productivity There's a Fly in My Soup: Can Insects Satisfy World Food Needs? Why Colorado and Washington Were Wise to Legalize Pot
Chapter 18: Public Finance: Expenditures and Taxes	13 States Raising Pay for Minimum-Wage Workers Bitcoin Only Worth What People Think It Is Worth Bitcoin: Why Businesses are Buying in, Despite Critics and Start-Up Woes Can Better Regulation Boost Growth? Crowdfunding Diplomacy: the Next Frontier for Government Economic Shocks Reverberate in World of Interconnected Trade Ties Freezing Paradise: an Update on Global Gender Equality Gender Pay and Leadership Gaps Are Real—and Impact Our Economy Interest in Pot Revenue at New High Panic Over US Tapering, China Growth Overdone, Insists IIF Should China Worry About a GDP Slowdown? Weakly Capitalized Banks Slowed Lending Recovery After Recession
Chapter 19: Antitrust Policy and Regulation	13 States Raising Pay for Minimum-Wage Workers Can Better Regulation Boost Growth? Freezing Paradise: an Update on Global Gender Equality Gender Pay and Leadership Gaps Are Real—and Impact Our Economy Is 'Amnesty' a Possibility Now? Reaching Out to Dropouts Weakly Capitalized Banks Slowed Lending Recovery After Recession
Chapter 20: Agriculture: Economics and Policy	13 States Raising Pay for Minimum-Wage Workers Austerity on the Side: EU Hits Restaurateurs with Olive Oil Law Economic Shocks Reverberate in World of Interconnected Trade Ties Interest in Pot Revenue at New High There's a Fly in My Soup: Can Insects Satisfy World Food Needs? Why Colorado and Washington Were Wise to Legalize Pot

Economics, 20/e By McConnell et al.	Annual Editions: Economics, 38/e
Chapter 21: Income Inequality, Poverty, and Discrimination	13 States Raising Pay for Minimum-Wage Worker After $75,000, Money Can't Buy Day-to-Day Happiness Can Better Regulation Boost Growth? Economic Shocks Reverberate in World of Interconnected Trade Ties Freezing Paradise: an Update on Global Gender Equality Gender Pay and Leadership Gaps Are Real—and Impact Our Economy Immigration and Happiness Immigration Reform Could Boost U.S. Economy Shortchanged Who Lives Longest?—Healthy, Wealthy—and Famous
Chapter 22: Health Care	Can Medicare Costs Be Tamed? Colorado in Jeopardy from Childhood Obesity Challenges Gender Pay and Leadership Gaps Are Real—and Impact Our Economy New Study Suggests eBooks Could Negatively Affect How We Comprehend What We Read Price Tag for Childhood Obesity: $19,000 Per Kid RPT-Obamacare Is on the Horizon, but Will Enough People Sign Up? Who Lives Longest?—Healthy, Wealthy—and Famous
Chapter 23: Immigration	Freezing Paradise: an Update on Global Gender Equality Gender Pay and Leadership Gaps Are Real—and Impact Our Economy Immigration and Happiness Immigration Reform Could Boost U.S. Economy Is 'Amnesty' a Possibility Now? Is the Border Secure? The Effect of Immigrants on U.S. Employment and Productivity Unemployment Rate
Chapter 24: An Introduction to Macroeconomics	Can Better Regulation Boost Growth? Economy Will Benefit from Immigration Reform The Effect of Immigrants on U.S. Employment and Productivity Unemployment Rate What Threat Do the Monetary Policies of Developed Nations Pose to Emerging Economies?
Chapter 25: Measuring Domestic Output and National Income	Can Better Regulation Boost Growth? Gender Pay and Leadership Gaps Are Real—and Impact Our Economy The Effect of Immigrants on U.S. Employment and Productivity Unemployment Rate What Threat Do the Monetary Policies of Developed Nations Pose to Emerging Economies?
Chapter 26: Economic Growth	Can Better Regulation Boost Growth? Economy Will Benefit from Immigration Reform Freezing Paradise: an Update on Global Gender Equality Gender Pay and Leadership Gaps Are Real—and Impact Our Economy Immigration Reform Could Boost U.S. Economy Reaching Out to Dropouts The Effect of Immigrants on U.S. Employment and Productivity The GED Test Gets a Makeover Unemployment Rate What Threat Do the Monetary Policies of Developed Nations Pose to Emerging Economies?
Chapter 27: Business Cycles, Unemployment, and Inflation	13 States Raising Pay for Minimum-Wage Workers Can Better Regulation Boost Growth? Can Medicare Costs Be Tamed? Crowdfunding Diplomacy: the Next Frontier for Government Economy Will Benefit from Immigration Reform Immigration and Happiness Immigration Reform Could Boost U.S. Economy Interest in Pot Revenue at New High Unemployment Rate Weakly Capitalized Banks Slowed Lending Recovery After Recession What Threat Do the Monetary Policies of Developed Nations Pose to Emerging Economies? Why Colorado and Washington Were Wise to Legalize Pot

Economics, 20/e By McConnell et al.	Annual Editions: Economics, 38/e
Chapter 28: Basic Macroeconomic Relationships	13 States Raising Pay for Minimum-Wage Workers Can Better Regulation Boost Growth? Can Medicare Costs Be Tamed? Crowdfunding Diplomacy: the Next Frontier for Government Economy Will Benefit from Immigration Reform Economic Shocks Reverberate in World of Interconnected Trade Ties Gender Pay and Leadership Gaps Are Real—and Impact Our Economy Immigration and Happiness Immigration Reform Could Boost U.S. Economy Interest in Pot Revenue at New High Unemployment Rate Should China Worry About a GDP Slowdown? Weakly Capitalized Banks Slowed Lending Recovery After Recession What Threat Do the Monetary Policies of Developed Nations Pose to Emerging Economies? Why Colorado and Washington Were Wise to Legalize Pot
Chapter 29: The Aggregate Expenditures Model	Can Better Regulation Boost Growth? Reaching Out to Dropouts Immigration and Happiness Immigration Reform Could Boost U.S. Economy The Effect of Immigrants on U.S. Employment and Productivity The GED Test Gets a Makeover What Threat Do the Monetary Policies of Developed Nations Pose to Emerging Economies?
Chapter 30: Aggregate Demand and Aggregate Supply	13 States Raising Pay for Minimum-Wage Workers Can Medicare Costs Be Tamed? Economy Will Benefit from Immigration Reform Immigration and Happiness Immigration Reform Could Boost U.S. Economy Interest in Pot Revenue at New High Is the Border Secure? Should China Worry About a GDP Slowdown? Unemployment Rate Virtual Health Care Gaining Ground What Threat Do the Monetary Policies of Developed Nations Pose to Emerging Economies? Why Colorado and Washington Were Wise to Legalize Pot
Chapter 31: Fiscal Policy, Deficits, and Debt	13 States Raising Pay for Minimum-Wage Workers Can Medicare Costs Be Tamed? Economy Will Benefit from Immigration Reform Immigration and Happiness Immigration Reform Could Boost U.S. Economy Interest in Pot Revenue at New High Unemployment Rate Weakly Capitalized Banks Slowed Lending Recovery After Recession What Threat Do the Monetary Policies of Developed Nations Pose to Emerging Economies? Why Colorado and Washington Were Wise to Legalize Pot
Chapter 32: Money, Banking, and Financial Institutions	13 States Raising Pay for Minimum-Wage Workers Can Medicare Costs Be Tamed? Economy Will Benefit from Immigration Reform Immigration and Happiness Immigration Reform Could Boost U.S. Economy Interest in Pot Revenue at New High Unemployment Rate What Threat Do the Monetary Policies of Developed Nations Pose to Emerging Economies? Why Colorado and Washington Were Wise to Legalize Pot
Chapter 33: Money Creation	Bitcoin Only Worth What People Think It Is Worth Bitcoin: Why Businesses are Buying in, Despite Critics and Start-Up Woes Can Better Regulation Boost Growth? Crowdfunding Diplomacy: the Next Frontier for Government Weakly Capitalized Banks Slowed Lending Recovery After Recession

Economics, 20/e By McConnell et al.	Annual Editions: Economics, 38/e
Chapter 34: Interest Rates and Monetary Policy	Can Better Regulation Boost Growth? Unemployment Rate Weakly Capitalized Banks Slowed Lending Recovery After Recession What Threat Do the Monetary Policies of Developed Nations Pose to Emerging Economies?
Chapter 35: Financial Economics	Bitcoin: Why Businesses are Buying in, Despite Critics and Start-Up Woes Can Better Regulation Boost Growth? Crowdfunding Diplomacy: the Next Frontier for Government Economic Shocks Reverberate in World of Interconnected Trade Ties Immigration Reform Could Boost U.S. Economy Weakly Capitalized Banks Slowed Lending Recovery After Recession What Threat Do the Monetary Policies of Developed Nations Pose to Emerging Economies?
Chapter 36: Extending the Analysis of Aggregate Supply	Austerity on the Side: EU Hits Restaurateurs with Olive Oil Law Economic Shocks Reverberate in World of Interconnected Trade Ties Panic Over US tapering, China Growth Overdone, Insists IIF Should China Worry About a GDP Slowdown? Unemployment Rate
Chapter 37: Current Issues in Macro Theory and Policy	13 States Raising Pay for Minimum-Wage Workers Bitcoin: Why Businesses are Buying in, Despite Critics and Start-Up Woes Can Better Regulation Boost Growth? Crowdfunding Diplomacy: the Next Frontier for Government The Effect of Immigrants on U.S. Employment and Productivity Freezing Paradise: an Update on Global Gender Equality Shortchanged Should China Worry About a GDP Slowdown? Unemployment Rate Weakly Capitalized Banks Slowed Lending Recovery After Recession What Threat Do the Monetary Policies of Developed Nations Pose to Emerging Economies? Why Colorado and Washington Were Wise to Legalize Pot
Chapter 38: International Trade	Bitcoin Only Worth What People Think It Is Worth Bitcoin: Why Businesses are Buying in, Despite Critics and Start-Up Woes Economic Shocks Reverberate in World of Interconnected Trade Ties Panic Over US tapering, China Growth Overdone, Insists IIF Should China Worry About a GDP Slowdown? What Threat Do the Monetary Policies of Developed Nations Pose to Emerging Economies?
Chapter 39: The Balance of Payments, Exchange Rates, and Trade Deficits	Bitcoin Only Worth What People Think It Is Worth Bitcoin: Why Businesses are Buying in, Despite Critics and Start-Up Woes Economic Shocks Reverberate in World of Interconnected Trade Ties Panic Over US tapering, China Growth Overdone, Insists IIF Should China Worry About a GDP Slowdown? What Threat Do the Monetary Policies of Developed Nations Pose to Emerging Economies?

This convenient guide matches the units in **Annual Editions: Economics, 38/e** with the corresponding chapters **Economics, 11/e by Slavin.**

Economics, 11/e By Slavin	Annual Editions: Economics, 38/e
Chapter 1: A Brief Economic History of the United States	
Chapter 2: Resource Utilization	Austerity on the Side: EU Hits Restaurateurs with Olive Oil Law Bitcoin Only Worth What People Think It Is Worth Can Medicare Costs Be Tamed? Crowdfunding Diplomacy: the Next Frontier for Government Economic Shocks Reverberate in World of Interconnected Trade Ties Gender Pay and Leadership Gaps Are Real—and Impact Our Economy There's a Fly in My Soup: Can Insects Satisfy World Food Needs? The Effect of Immigrants on U.S. Employment and Productivity
Chapter 3: The Mixed Economy	Austerity on the Side: EU Hits Restaurateurs with Olive Oil Law Panic Over US tapering, China Growth Overdone, Insists IIF Should China Worry About a GDP Slowdown? What Threat Do the Monetary Policies of Developed Nations Pose to Emerging Economies?
Chapter 4: Supply and Demand	13 States Raising Pay for Minimum-Wage Workers Bitcoin Only Worth What People Think It Is Worth Can Medicare Costs Be Tamed? Crowdfunding Diplomacy: the Next Frontier for Government Gender Pay and Leadership Gaps Are Real—and Impact Our Economy Interest in Pot Revenue at New High Price Tag for Childhood Obesity: $19,000 Per Kid Why Colorado and Washington Were Wise to Legalize Pot
Chapter 5: The Household Consumption Sector	After $75,000, Money Can't Buy Day-to-Day Happiness New Study Suggests eBooks Could Negatively Affect How We Comprehend What We Read Price Tag for Childhood Obesity: $19,000 Per Kid There's a Fly in My Soup: Can Insects Satisfy World Food Needs? Who Lives Longest?—Healthy, Wealthy—and Famous
Chapter 6: The Business Investment Sector	13 States Raising Pay for Minimum-Wage Workers Can Better Regulation Boost Growth? Crowdfunding Diplomacy: the Next Frontier for Government Economy Will Benefit from Immigration Reform Interest in Pot Revenue at New High Unemployment Rate Weakly Capitalized Banks Slowed Lending Recovery After Recession What Threat Do the Monetary Policies of Developed Nations Pose to Emerging Economies? Why Colorado and Washington Were Wise to Legalize Pot
Chapter 7: The Government Sector	13 States Raising Pay for Minimum-Wage Workers Can Better Regulation Boost Growth? Can Medicare Costs Be Tamed? Crowdfunding Diplomacy: the Next Frontier for Government Economy Will Benefit from Immigration Reform Economic Shocks Reverberate in World of Interconnected Trade Ties Gender Pay and Leadership Gaps Are Real—and Impact Our Economy Immigration and Happiness Immigration Reform Could Boost U.S. Economy Interest in Pot Revenue at New High Unemployment Rate Should China Worry About a GDP Slowdown? Weakly Capitalized Banks Slowed Lending Recovery After Recession What Threat Do the Monetary Policies of Developed Nations Pose to Emerging Economies? Why Colorado and Washington Were Wise to Legalize Pot
Chapter 8: The Export Import Sector	Can Better Regulation Boost Growth? Reaching Out to Dropouts Immigration and Happiness Immigration Reform Could Boost U.S. Economy The Effect of Immigrants on U.S. Employment and Productivity The GED Test Gets a Makeover What Threat Do the Monetary Policies of Developed Nations Pose to Emerging Economies?

Economics, 11/e By Slavin	Annual Editions: Economics, 38/e
Chapter 9: Gross Domestic Product	13 States Raising Pay for Minimum-Wage Workers Can Medicare Costs Be Tamed? Economy Will Benefit from Immigration Reform Immigration and Happiness Immigration Reform Could Boost U.S. Economy Interest in Pot Revenue at New High Is the Border Secure? Should China Worry About a GDP Slowdown? Unemployment Rate Virtual Health Care Gaining Ground What Threat Do the Monetary Policies of Developed Nations Pose to Emerging Economies? Why Colorado and Washington Were Wise to Legalize Pot
Chapter 10: Economic Fluctuations, Unemployment, and Inflation	Can Better Regulation Boost Growth? Economy Will Benefit from Immigration Reform Freezing Paradise: an Update on Global Gender Equality Gender Pay and Leadership Gaps Are Real—and Impact Our Economy Immigration Reform Could Boost U.S. Economy Reaching Out to Dropouts The Effect of Immigrants on U.S. Employment and Productivity The GED Test Gets a Makeover Unemployment Rate What Threat Do the Monetary Policies of Developed Nations Pose to Emerging Economies?
Chapter 11: Classical and Keynesian Economics	
Chapter 12: Fiscal Policy and the National Debt	13 States Raising Pay for Minimum-Wage Workers Can Medicare Costs Be Tamed? Economy Will Benefit from Immigration Reform Immigration and Happiness Immigration Reform Could Boost U.S. Economy Interest in Pot Revenue at New High Unemployment Rate Weakly Capitalized Banks Slowed Lending Recovery After Recession What Threat Do the Monetary Policies of Developed Nations Pose to Emerging Economies? Why Colorado and Washington Were Wise to Legalize Pot
Chapter 13: Money and Banking	Bitcoin Only Worth What People Think It Is Worth Bitcoin: Why Businesses are Buying in, Despite Critics and Start-Up Woes Can Better Regulation Boost Growth? Crowdfunding Diplomacy: the Next Frontier for Government Weakly Capitalized Banks Slowed Lending Recovery After Recession
Chapter 14: The Federal Reserve and Monetary Policy	Can Better Regulation Boost Growth? Unemployment Rate Weakly Capitalized Banks Slowed Lending Recovery After Recession What Threat Do the Monetary Policies of Developed Nations Pose to Emerging Economies?
Chapter 15: A Century of Economic Theory	
Chapter 16: Economic Growth and Productivity	Can Better Regulation Boost Growth? Economy Will Benefit from Immigration Reform Freezing Paradise: an Update on Global Gender Equality Gender Pay and Leadership Gaps Are Real—and Impact Our Economy Immigration Reform Could Boost U.S. Economy Reaching Out to Dropouts The Effect of Immigrants on U.S. Employment and Productivity The GED Test Gets a Makeover Unemployment Rate What Threat Do the Monetary Policies of Developed Nations Pose to Emerging Economies?

Economics, 11/e By Slavin	Annual Editions: Economics, 38/e
Chapter 17: Demand, Supply, and Equilibrium	13 States Raising Pay for Minimum-Wage Workers Bitcoin Only Worth What People Think It Is Worth Can Medicare Costs Be Tamed? Crowdfunding Diplomacy: the Next Frontier for Government Interest in Pot Revenue at New High Price Tag for Childhood Obesity: $19,000 Per Kid
Chapter 18: The Price Elasticities of Demand and Supply	Austerity on the Side: EU Hits Restaurateurs with Olive Oil Law Bitcoin Only Worth What People Think It Is Worth Can Medicare Costs Be Tamed? Crowdfunding Diplomacy: the Next Frontier for Government Interest in Pot Revenue at New High Price Tag for Childhood Obesity: $19,000 Per Kid Why Colorado and Washington Were Wise to Legalize Pot
Chapter 19: Theory of Consumer Behavior	13 States Raising Pay for Minimum-Wage Workers Bitcoin Only Worth What People Think It Is Worth Can Better Regulation Boost Growth? Crowdfunding Diplomacy: the Next Frontier for Government Freezing Paradise: an Update on Global Gender Equality Gender Pay and Leadership Gaps Are Real—and Impact Our Economy Interest in Pot Revenue at New High New Study Suggests eBooks Could Negatively Affect How We Comprehend What We Read Panic Over US Tapering, China Growth Overdone, Insists IIF
Chapter 20: Cost	13 States Raising Pay for Minimum-Wage Workers Can Better Regulation Boost Growth? Freezing Paradise: an Update on Global Gender Equality Gender Pay and Leadership Gaps Are Real—and Impact Our Economy Is 'Amnesty' a Possibility Now? Reaching Out to Dropouts Weakly Capitalized Banks Slowed Lending Recovery After Recession
Chapter 21: Profit, Loss, and Perfect Competition	Can Better Regulation Boost Growth? Freezing Paradise: an Update on Global Gender Equality Gender Pay and Leadership Gaps Are Real—and Impact Our Economy Is 'Amnesty' a Possibility Now? Reaching Out to Dropouts Weakly Capitalized Banks Slowed Lending Recovery After Recession
Chapter 22: Monopoly	After $75,000, Money Can't Buy Day-to-Day Happiness Crowdfunding Diplomacy: the Next Frontier for Government Interest in Pot Revenue at New High RPT-Obamacare Is on the Horizon, but Will Enough People Sign Up? Virtual Health Care Gaining Ground
Chapter 23: Monopolistic Competition	Crowdfunding Diplomacy: the Next Frontier for Government Interest in Pot Revenue at New High RPT-Obamacare Is on the Horizon, but Will Enough People Sign Up? Virtual Health Care Gaining Ground Why Colorado and Washington Were Wise to Legalize Pot
Chapter 24: Oligopoly	
Chapter 25: Corporate Mergers and Antitrust	13 States Raising Pay for Minimum-Wage Workers Can Better Regulation Boost Growth? Freezing Paradise: an Update on Global Gender Equality Gender Pay and Leadership Gaps Are Real—and Impact Our Economy Is 'Amnesty' a Possibility Now? Reaching Out to Dropouts Weakly Capitalized Banks Slowed Lending Recovery After Recession

Economics, 11/e By Slavin	Annual Editions: Economics, 38/e
Chapter 26: Demand in the Factor Market	13 States Raising Pay for Minimum-Wage Workers Economy Will Benefit from Immigration Reform Freezing Paradise: an Update on Global Gender Equality Gender Pay and Leadership Gaps Are Real—and Impact Our Economy Reaching Out to Dropouts Shortchanged The Effect of Immigrants on U.S. Employment and Productivity The GED Test Gets a Makeover Who Lives Longest?—Healthy, Wealthy—and Famous
Chapter 27: Labor Unions	13 States Raising Pay for Minimum-Wage Workers Freezing Paradise: an Update on Global Gender Equality Gender Pay and Leadership Gaps Are Real—and Impact Our Economy Shortchanged The Effect of Immigrants on U.S. Employment and Productivity
Chapter 28: Labor Markets and Wage Rates	Freezing Paradise: an Update on Global Gender Equality Gender Pay and Leadership Gaps Are Real—and Impact Our Economy Neighborhoods Benefit From Immigrants Immigration and Happiness Immigration Reform Could Boost U.S. Economy Is 'Amnesty' a Possibility Now? Is the Border Secure? The Effect of Immigrants on U.S. Employment and Productivity Unemployment Rate
Chapter 29: Rent, Interest, and Profit	13 States Raising Pay for Minimum-Wage Workers Economy Will Benefit from Immigration Reform Freezing Paradise: an Update on Global Gender Equality Gender Pay and Leadership Gaps Are Real—and Impact Our Economy Shortchanged The Effect of Immigrants on U.S. Employment and Productivity
Chapter 30: Income Distribution and Poverty	13 States Raising Pay for Minimum-Wage Workers After $75,000, Money Can't Buy Day-to-Day Happiness Freezing Paradise: an Update on Global Gender Equality Gender Pay and Leadership Gaps Are Real—and Impact Our Economy Immigration and Happiness Immigration Reform Could Boost U.S. Economy Is 'Amnesty' a Possibility Now? Is the Border Secure? Reaching Out to Dropouts The Effect of Immigrants on U.S. Employment and Productivity The GED Test Gets a Makeover Unemployment Rate
Chapter 31: International Trade	Bitcoin Only Worth What People Think It Is Worth Bitcoin: Why Businesses are Buying in, Despite Critics and Start-Up Woes Economic Shocks Reverberate in World of Interconnected Trade Ties Panic over US Tapering, China Growth Overdone, Insists IIF Should China Worry About a GDP Slowdown? What Threat Do the Monetary Policies of Developed Nations Pose to Emerging Economies?
Chapter 32: International Finance	Bitcoin: Why Businesses are Buying in, Despite Critics and Start-Up Woes Can Better Regulation Boost Growth? Crowdfunding Diplomacy: the Next Frontier for Government Economic Shocks Reverberate in World of Interconnected Trade Ties Economy Will Benefit from Immigration Reform Freezing Paradise: an Update on Global Gender Equality What Threat Do the Monetary Policies of Developed Nations Pose to Emerging Economies?

Topic Guide

Banking industry

Bitcoin Only Worth What People Think It Is Worth
Weakly Capitalized Banks Slowed Lending Recovery After
    Recession
What Threat Do the Monetary Policies of Developed Nations Pose to
    Emerging Economies?

Chinese economy

Economic Shocks Reverberate in World of Interconnected Trade Ties
Panic over US tapering, China Growth Overdone, Insists IIF
Should China Worry About a GDP Slowdown?
What Threat Do the Monetary Policies of Developed Nations Pose to
    Emerging Economies?

Common resource problem

Bitcoin Only Worth What People Think It Is Worth
Can Medicare Costs Be Tamed?
Crowdfunding Diplomacy: the Next Frontier for Government
Economy Will Benefit from Immigration Reform
Immigration and Happiness
Immigration Reform Could Boost U.S. Economy
Interest in Pot Revenue at New High
Is 'Amnesty' a Possibility Now?
New Study Suggests eBooks Could Negatively Affect How We
    Comprehend What We Read
Reaching Out to Dropouts
RPT-Obamacare Is on the Horizon, but Will Enough People
    Sign Up?
The GED Test Gets a Makeover
There's a Fly in My Soup: Can Insects Satisfy World Food Needs?

Competition

Austerity on the Side: EU Hits Restaurateurs with Olive Oil Law
Can Medicare Costs Be Tamed?
Colorado in Jeopardy from Childhood Obesity Challenges
Crowdfunding Diplomacy: the Next Frontier for Government
Economic Shocks Reverberate in World of Interconnected Trade Ties
Immigration and Happiness
Price Tag for Childhood Obesity: $19,000 Per Kid
Reaching Out to Dropouts
Should China Worry About a GDP Slowdown?
The Effect of Immigrants on U.S. Employment and Productivity
The GED Test Gets a Makeover
There's a Fly in My Soup: Can Insects Satisfy World Food Needs?
Unemployment Rate
Virtual Health Care Gaining Ground
What Threat Do the Monetary Policies of Developed Nations Pose to
    Emerging Economies?

Consumers

After $75,000, Money Can't Buy Day-to-Day Happiness
Freezing Paradise: an Update on Global Gender Equality
RPT-Obamacare Is on the Horizon, but Will Enough People Sign Up?
Unemployment Rate
Who Lives Longest?—Healthy, Wealthy—and Famous

Corporate responsibility

Can Better Regulation Boost Growth?
Freezing Paradise: an Update on Global Gender Equality
Unemployment Rate
What Threat Do the Monetary Policies of Developed Nations Pose to
    Emerging Economies?

Cost-benefit analysis

Can Medicare Costs Be Tamed?
Is 'Amnesty' a Possibility Now?
Immigration and Happiness
Immigration Reform Could Boost U.S. Economy
Is the Border Secure?
Price Tag for Childhood Obesity: $19,000 Per Kid
Reaching Out to Dropouts
RPT-Obamacare Is on the Horizon, but Will Enough People Sign Up?
Shortchanged
The GED Test Gets a Makeover
There's a Fly in My Soup: Can Insects Satisfy World Food Needs?
Virtual Health Care Gaining Ground
What Threat Do the Monetary Policies of Developed Nations Pose to
    Emerging Economies?
Who Lives Longest?—Healthy, Wealthy—and Famous

Discrimination

Can Medicare Costs Be Tamed?
Freezing Paradise: an Update on Global Gender Equality
Gender Pay and Leadership Gaps Are Real—and Impact Our
    Economy
Is 'Amnesty' a Possibility Now?
Is the Border Secure?
Price Tag for Childhood Obesity: $19,000 Per Kid
Reaching Out to Dropouts
RPT-Obamacare Is on the Horizon, but Will Enough People Sign Up?
Shortchanged
The Effect of Immigrants on U.S. Employment and Productivity
The GED Test Gets a Makeover
Unemployment Rate
Who Lives Longest?—Healthy, Wealthy—and Famous

Energy and the environment

Austerity on the Side: EU Hits Restaurateurs with Olive Oil Law
Bitcoin: Why Businesses are Buying in, Despite Critics and Start-Up Woes
Can Better Regulation Boost Growth?
Should China Worry About a GDP Slowdown?
The GED Test Gets a Makeover
There's a Fly in My Soup: Can Insects Satisfy World Food Needs?
Virtual Health Care Gaining Ground
Who Lives Longest?—Healthy, Wealthy—and Famous

Entrepreneurs

13 States Raising Pay for Minimum-Wage Workers
Crowdfunding Diplomacy: the Next Frontier for Government
Economy Will Benefit from Immigration Reform
Unemployment Rate
Why Colorado and Washington Were Wise to Legalize Pot

Federal budget deficit

Austerity on the Side: EU Hits Restaurateurs with Olive Oil Law
Colorado in Jeopardy from Childhood Obesity Challenges
RPT-Obamacare Is on the Horizon, but Will Enough People Sign Up?
Shortchanged
Should China Worry About a GDP Slowdown?
The Effect of Immigrants on U.S. Employment and Productivity
Unemployment Rate

Fiscal policy

13 States Raising Pay for Minimum-Wage Workers
Can Better Regulation Boost Growth?

Unit 1

UNIT

Introduction

Prepared by: Sudip Ghosh, *Penn State University—Berks*

Why it is important to study economics? When the economy does well we all benefit and when it falters we all suffer. Economics is about how people choose. The choices we make influence our lives and those of others. Everything we do has an opportunity cost.

This unit focuses on varied topics such as medicare costs, income and happiness, wage equity, and effects of ebooks on learning and comprehension, Most of these topics are health and wellness related and explore an age old question:

how much money will make you content? The magic number turns out to be $75,000, marginal increase in income does not add to happiness but marginal decline in income causes distress. Furthermore, women constitute about 50 percent of the work force. In Northern European countries not only wages are equal but also other amenities. It is quite easy to get distracted on the Internet, and ebooks are certainly not an exception which poses learning challenge for people who find difficulty in focusing.

Article   Prepared by: Sudip Ghosh, *Penn State University—Berks*

Can Medicare Costs Be Tamed?

If spending isn't contained soon, it may spell trouble for taxpayers and the US economy.

MARK TRUMBULL

Learning Outcomes

After reading this article, you will be able to:

- Understand the challenges facing Medicare and the role of the government to boost competition in the healthcare industry.

- Explain reasons for healthcare being so expensive.

For a quick glimpse of America's health-care challenge, consider this: The nation spent $8,233 per person on medical care in 2010—more than twice the average of other advanced economies, including Germany, Britain, Canada, and Japan.

America doesn't have bad health care, judging by life expectancies that are on par with other nations, but it does have notably *expensive* health care.

And a lot of the payment burden rests on the US government, through entitlement programs including Medicare for seniors and Medicaid for the poor. If this problem isn't addressed as baby boomers retire, it's a recipe for deep trouble for taxpayers and the US economy.

Medical costs are high and rising for reasons that go beyond the demographics of an aging nation. At the individual level, doctors and patients together are opting for a greater volume of health-care services. Some of that, economists say, reflects people buying improved health care as their incomes rise. Some reflects wasteful decisions that don't improve health outcomes.

And beyond the number of patients treated and the volume of care each receives, researchers see another factor: Hospitals and doctors in the United States have a pricing power that they simply lack in other nations.

"The reason the US spends so much more per capita and as a percentage of GDP than other countries is *not* because we do that many more services. . . . It's because our prices are higher than anybody else's," says Robert Berenson, a health-care expert at the Urban Institute in Washington. "Physicians' incomes are at the high end. . . . Nursing income is at the high end. Hospital executive salaries are way over the high end."

Health care at all levels, from a consumer's co-payment to the billions spent by government, now accounts for 18 percent of gross domestic product—almost $1 in every $5. That's up from 7 percent of GDP in 1970. Several in-depth studies have concluded that as much as one-third of overall US health-care spending—and possibly of Medicare spending—is wasteful and does nothing to improve the quality of care.

That doesn't mean it's easy to cut costs 30 percent or more.

"There is no silver bullet" solution, says Elliott Fisher, a health policy expert at Geisel School of Medicine at Dartmouth College in Hanover, N.H. But "solving the fiscal crisis that is posed by rising health-care costs is incredibly important."

To a large degree, all the budgetary bluster and hand-wringing by politicians this year boils down to a simple but vexing question: How should the US reform these programs that millions rely on, so that benefits are provided without breaking the nation's bank?

Yes, the fiscal debates also include important attention to tax reform and spending on everything from defense to farm subsidies. But entitlements, particularly in health care, are the elephant in the room.

The outlook isn't all financial gloom. The growth of Medicare costs, per beneficiary, has slowed in the past few years. And although there's no guarantee that trend will continue, many health policy experts say tallies of waste or overpricing are evidence that there's considerable room for restraining costs.

Mr. Berenson and some of his colleagues at the Urban Institute have proposed an action menu that could cut projected Medicare spending by some $300 billion (a 4 percent cut) or more over the next decade, with minimal impact on benefits.

Some steps are as simple as saying "no" to traditional practices, such as Medicare payments that indirectly support medical education. While still investing in the most-needed doctor training, the US government could save some $50 billion over 10 years from that step alone, Berenson's report estimated.

The Entitlement Time Bomb

Before delving deeper into potential solutions, though, it's important to set this issue of entitlement reform in context. Why is it so important? How big do the changes need to be?

The very word "entitlement" is controversial. To some Americans it carries the pejorative notion of people mooching off the federal government, while others grow defensive about benefits they feel they've paid for.

Like it or not, though, "entitlements" is the ubiquitous term for some very costly programs that channel benefits from the government to ordinary Americans. And the fact is, the typical Medicare beneficiary, despite contributing payroll taxes during working years and premiums during retirement, doesn't come close to covering the whole tab.

Medicare, with 50 million beneficiaries and rising to 80 million by 2037, is the biggest "entitlement bomb" in the federal budget. But it's not the only one. Social Security is also projected to stake a rising claim on the nation's financial resources over the next decade and beyond.

Medicaid, though less talked about, is an important piece of the puzzle. It's smaller in scale than Social Security or Medicare, aiming at a narrower slice of the population. But as the safety net for the poor, it increasingly serves as the backstop when seniors run out of money for costs not covered by Medicare. Medicaid spending has been rising steadily, and options for cost savings may be few.

With the two political parties split on whether more tax revenue should be part of the fix, it's not clear whether President Obama and Congress will make any legislative headway toward entitlement reform this year.

A report last year by the nonpartisan Congressional Budget Office (CBO) put the consequences of political inaction in sharp relief, noting that the fiscal hole gets deeper the longer America waits. In one scenario reflecting status-quo fiscal policies, corrective action taken this year (tax hikes or spending cuts, or both) would need to equal more than 4 percent of GDP through 2037 in order to keep the national debt stable as a share of GDP.

That's big. But if politicians were to postpone action for a dozen years, until 2025, the CBO says the tax or spending changes would need to be bigger still—twice as large to reach the same debt target by 2037.

How to Tame the Medicare Beast?

The same forecasts show how central healthcare entitlements are to America's rising debt challenge.

During that period, from today through 2037, health-care entitlements alone could nearly double in size to 10.4 percent of GDP, according to the CBO. Social Security, too, is on track to expand in size to 6 percent of GDP, compared with 5 percent today. Yet overall federal tax revenues currently look set to total only about 19 percent of GDP.

Sherry Glied, a professor of health policy at Columbia University in New York, says the options for cost control fall into three broad categories. The first is to try to nudge prices downward, such as by tinkering with government payment rates to care providers. The second is to try to change the way care is delivered, in ways that give providers incentives to improve quality and reduce costs. The third is to take the government off the hook, by shifting more of the cost burden to consumers.

In the end, it may be that a mix of all three is deployed. But Ms. Glied argues that, because the government has focused on Option 1 in recent years, the big effort for now should go toward Option 2.

Medicare Facts

15% of Americans are enrolled as of 2010.

It'll be **21%** by 2030.

Average Medicare participant paid **$4,241** out-of-pocket for health care 2010.

Share of beneficiaries' income used to cover out-of-pocket health-care expenses has jumped: **12%** in 1997 versus **16%** in 2006.

Medicare payroll taxes, deducted from worker paychecks, cover **37%** of program costs. The US general fund, along with enrollee premiums, pays most of the rest.

Eight million, or 17% of participants, are enrolled because of disability, not age.

Share of enrollees with annual incomes higher than $50,000: **15%**. Share with annual incomes no higher than twice the official level of poverty: **47%**. Share that also qualifies for the Medicaid program for the poor: **17%**.

60% of Medicare spending is incurred by **10%** of high-needs patients.

Graphic: RICH CLABAUGH/STAFF
SOURCE: Kaiser Family Foundation

Already, Mr. Obama's 2010 Affordable Care Act contains some initiatives on this track. The Center for Medicare & Medicaid Innovation, for one, is working to spread promising models of care and cost control.

But health experts say more steps will be needed. Among the many new ideas, a few might have broad—but hard to quantify—impacts on the behavior of health-market participants like physicians, hospital administrators, and patients.

Here are prominent examples that may have potential to gather bipartisan support:

1. Pay for Quality, not Quantity of Services

In Medicare's traditional "fee for service" model, the financial incentives tilt toward doing that extra test or procedure when in doubt. Reform proponents say the better way involves approaches that pay increasingly for the quality of patient care, rather than its quantity—and which offer incentives for teamwork and information-sharing among health-care professionals.

"That's the single most important thing we could do," says John Rother, president of the National Coalition on Health Care, which represents a wide range of stakeholder groups.

Some proponents urge payment reforms—both within and outside Medicare—that encourage providers to accept a single in-advance fee for each person in their care. If the organization keeps costs down, it pockets a higher profit. If its care is excellent, more customers will come through the doors. This is the "accountable care organization" model, which is getting a test run in Medicare under the Affordable Care Act.

2. Use Antitrust Law to Boost Competition

Whether in or out of Medicare, the idea of giving providers incentives to hold costs down works best when providers have to compete with one another for business. But in many markets, competition among health-care providers is relatively limited—partly because of a trend of consolidation among hospitals as well as insurers.

Leemore Dafny, a Northwestern University economist who's serving as deputy director of health care and antitrust at the Federal Trade Commission, says it's not too late for antitrust efforts to play an important role in fostering competitive markets for health care.

"The last couple of years have seen a turn toward more successful enforcement" efforts, she says.

3. Engage the Consumer

Many reform proposals hinge on the idea of enlisting the consumer to be more cost-conscious.

For instance, when Medicare beneficiaries buy supplemental "Medi-gap" insurance, they are largely shielded from out-of-pocket costs—leaving little financial incentive to restrain their use of medical services.

The Urban Institute's Berenson suggests a rule change for these policies, so that policyholders would have to pay at least half of the first $4,950 in Medicare expenses. Backers of this general approach add a caveat, though: The challenge is that cost-conscious consumers may forgo needed as well as unneeded care.

Whatever paths are pursued, Medicare is sure to keep evolving.

"We've been making tough choices in the Medicare program since five years after it started," Glied says, "and we're never going to stop."

Critical Thinking

1. What steps can be taken to meet the challenges facing Medicare?

2. If baby boomers continue to retire at an increasing rate will Medicare breakdown?

3. How can the consumer be engaged to achieve needed reform?

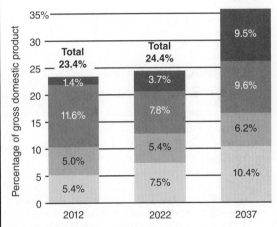

Growing Strain of Entitlements

In one plausible scenario of where current policies are headed, federal spending surges over the next 25 years, to take up about 36 percent of the US economy—a shift that many economists say would slow the nation's economic progress. The rise stems largely from health-care entitlements and a related jump in interest payments.

- Interest on debt
- Other federal spending
- Social Security
- Health-care entitlements*

Includes Medicare, Medicaid, CHIP, and Obamacare subsidies for individual insurance

Graphic: RICH CLABAUGH/STAFF

SOURCE: Congressional Budget Office, 2012 long-term budget outlook "alternative fiscal scenario"

Create Central

www.mhhe.com/createcentral

Internet References

www.pbs.org/newshour/rundown/2013/04/top-five-ways-the-presidents-budget-would-change-medicare.html

www.modernhealthcare.com/article/20130410/NEWS/304109960

http://articles.latimes.com/2013/apr/11/news/la-ol-medicare-obamacare-president-obama-paul-ryan-20130410

www.csmonitor.com/USA/DC-Decoder/2013/0402/Taming-Medicare-costs-What-are-the-options

www.csmonitor.com/Business/2013/0508/New-report-reveals-stunning-disparities-in-health-care-costs

Article   Prepared by: Sudip Ghosh, *Penn State University—Berks*

After $75,000, Money Can't Buy Day-to-Day Happiness

But the more people make, the better they feel about their lives overall, study found.

JENIFER GOODWIN

Learning Outcomes

After reading this article, you will be able to:

- Explain the relationship between money and emotional happiness.

- Understand the optimum sum one needs to be emotionally fulfilled.

Money can help buy happiness—at least if you're bringing in about $75,000 a year, new research shows. While happiness increases along with annual household incomes up to about $75,000, beyond that, earning more money has no effect on day-to-day contentment, according to the study.

But that doesn't mean you should give up trying to get that promotion. While making more won't help your emotional state on any given day, people who had household incomes above $75,000 *were* more apt to say they were satisfied overall with their life.

Those who made, say, $120,000, reported more satisfaction with their lives and had a higher assessment of their life overall than those who made less, while those who made $160,000 evaluated their lives even better still.

"It's really important to recognize that the word 'happiness' covers a lot of ground," said study author Angus Deaton, a professor of economics and international affairs at Princeton University. "There is your overall evaluation of how your life is going, while the other has to do more with emotional well-being at the moment. Higher incomes don't seem to have any effect on well-being after around $75,000, whereas your evaluation of your life keeps going up along with income."

The study is in the Sept. 6 early edition of the *Proceedings of the National Academy of Sciences*.

Researchers used data from the Gallup-Healthways Well-Being Index, which surveyed 450,000 Americans in 2008 and 2009 about their household income, emotional state during the prior day and overall feelings about their life and well-being.

Both measures of happiness are getting at something different, Deaton noted. You might be feeling blue or unhappy one day because your boss hassled you or you got a speeding ticket, but overall, you think life is going pretty well.

Conversely, you might have felt happy, even joyful, on an outing with your friends and family, but are overall not satisfied with your life or the direction it's going.

So which measure of happiness matters more?

That's a philosophical question and perhaps one only the individual can answer, Deaton said. "That's a really deep, hard question. [Both measures] are important. But if you're unhappy now, the fact your life may be going well doesn't make up for that."

Social scientists and psychologists have long grappled with how to measure happiness, said James Maddux, a psychology professor at George Mason University in Fairfax, Va., who was not involved with the study.

The new study does a good job teasing apart the different aspects of emotional well-being, including more immediate emotions vs. bigger-picture life evaluations, Maddux said.

"This study is consistent with a lot of other studies on the relationship between income and happiness or overall life satisfaction," Maddux said. "What other studies have also shown is that money matters up to a point. But after a certain point, having additional money doesn't make people like their lives better or feel better about themselves on a day to day basis."

This holds true in other countries around the world as well, he noted. Once per capita GDP rises to a point in which people are no longer struggling to meet basic needs such as food, clothing, shelter and healthcare, additional increases in overall national wealth don't seem to make much of a difference in happiness, Maddux said.

Maddux urged America's beleaguered workers not to get too hung up on the $75,000 figure. That income level can mean very different things depending on how many people are in the family, what sorts of financial responsibilities you have and where you live, he said.

"$75,000 is not a magical figure people need to achieve to be at their happiest," Maddux said. "The point is there is a threshold at which people probably are not going to be substantially happier if they keep making more money."

In 2008, average U.S household income was about $71,500, while the median—or the point at which half of incomes are higher and half are lower—was $52,000. The average skews higher than the median because of a few very high incomes, Deaton explained.

While people with household incomes of more than $75,000 probably won't feel an enduring happiness boost if they are able to earn more, losing substantial income would likely not be good for their emotional well being, the study suggested. As income dropped, respondents reported declining happiness and increased sadness and stress.

And, according to the study, poverty exacerbated the emotional impact of negative life events such as illness and divorce. Nor did the poor get as much of a happiness boost from weekends as those who were better-off, according to the researchers.

"Life is unfair for the poor in all sorts of dimensions," Deaton said.

More Information

The U.S. National Institute of Mental Health has more information on anxiety and other mental health conditions.

Critical Thinking

1. What happens when income increases significantly?
2. Does a vast sum of money give you unlimited happiness?

Create Central

www.mhhe.com/createcentral

Internet References

www.time.com/time/magazine/article/0,9171,2019628,00.html

http://blogs.wsj.com/wealth/2010/09/07/the-perfect-salary-for -happiness-75000-a-year/

http://lifehacker.com/5632191/75000-is-the-perfect-salary-for-happiness

Article Prepared by: Sudip Ghosh, *Penn State University—Berks*

Immigration and Happiness

BRYCE BYTHEWAY

Learning Outcomes

After reading this article, you will be able to:

- Understand the psychology of immigration.
- Discuss the relationship between happiness and upward mobility.

Many immigrants dream of improved lives in their adopted country, but the reality is not quite as majestic. While life in wealthier countries may be better, particularly when one's financial situation is improved, immigrants often discover that their new life has not made them happier.

New research published in the Oxford Journal *Migration Studies* suggests that immigrants looking for a better economic situation are often unlikely to achieve greater happiness in their new country. Using data on 42,000 people from the European Social Survey, sociologist David Bartram from England's University of Leicester explained how immigration to a wealthier country often resulted in a lower economic status for the immigrant, taking away from the immigrant's overall happiness.

Happiness Defined

Before continuing further into the study, it would be important to take a step back and define happiness. In an article on *Quartz,* Bartram explained the means of defining happiness for the purpose of the study, "In economic terms, what matters for happiness is the way one compares oneself to others. If one's income rises in line with the incomes of others, relative position does not change, and so happiness remains unchanged as well." Bartram further explained, "Even when income rises significantly, leading to upward mobility, people often adjust their reference groups, comparing to others at a higher level rather than deriving satisfaction from comparing themselves to a stable reference group."

The Outcomes

Bartram's research examined immigrants moving from Eastern European countries, and compared them to those who remained in their homeland (stayers). Immigrants overall tended to be happier than stayers, but the analysis indicated that many immigrants were already happier before they immigrated. For most of the countries analyzed, the immigrants' level of happiness varied little, but there were a few exceptions both positive and negative to this conclusion.

The experiences of the immigrants differed depending on their country of origin. Romania and Russia, for example, gained much more happiness post migration than any other immigrant group studied. This outcome is attributed to the fact that Romania and Russia have a much lower average of happiness among their citizens. For many of these immigrants, just the opportunity to live elsewhere seemed to increase their overall level of happiness.

Polish migrants, on the other hand, experienced a significant decrease in happiness when immigrating to Western Europe. The study shows that a high level of happiness already exists within Poland, similar to that of many Western European countries. A large gap appears when comparing the happiness levels of Polish immigrants and stayers, adding to the argument that immigrating to a wealthier country does not always increase happiness.

Roadblocks in the Pursuit of Happiness

Overall the study shows that immigrating to a wealthier country doesn't necessarily increase one's level of happiness, in fact on average it shows very little change. If this is true then the question arises; why don't immigrants experience increased happiness? Bartram refers back to his definition of happiness, how people compare themselves to others, to explain the phenomenon.

Upon arriving in their newly adopted country, immigrants compare themselves to the stayers and instantly recognize and rejoice in their improved life. As time passes they start to compare themselves to the natives, and the realization hits that they are not as well off as those around them. Jobs and higher wages that seemed so attractive at first are now realized to be inferior to those of their neighbors. Gradually, many immigrants start to realize that their social status has dropped, and the once majestically high wages are, in reality quite low, after inflation has been added to the equation.

Other contributors arise as they continue to compare themselves to the natives; many immigrants lose happiness as they experience prejudices and discrimination from the native population. Many become frustrated when their experience and qualifications are not recognized within their adopted country, and they are forced to work jobs that they are over qualified to do, leaving many aspirations to be unsatisfied.

The root of unhappiness, it seems, stems from comparing yourself to those around you.

A factor worthy of consideration is the reason for international immigration: does the immigrant move seeking his own happiness, or does he do it to support his family? Immigration involves significant upheaval of one's life, and the drawbacks are many. Adapting to new surroundings and culture, as well as the effects that immigration has on relationships, both old and new, can lead to a decrease in happiness. If one's immigration is the result of an attempt to support loved ones, do the increased wages and better economy outweigh the drawbacks associated with family separation?

Upward Mobility

It is also interesting to note that just as immigrating to a wealthier nation does not necessarily increase happiness, neither does moving upward on the social ladder. Immigrants (as well as natives) who find that they are accepted, experience a significant increase of income, and are able to move to an increased social status, often do not experience the increase in happiness they expected either. Human nature is to compare yourself to those around you; an increase in social status often begins with an increased level of happiness as you continue to compare

yourself to your previous counterparts, be it stayers or those of a lower social status. But as one accustoms himself to his new surroundings the bar for happiness is raised, and many don't experience a long-term increase of happiness.

How do we Achieve Happiness?

Happiness, it seems, is an ever-changing idea that is hard to hold on to. It requires more than a simple status change or a wealthier nation. It appears that it really depends upon one's priorities. Once people's basic needs are secured, then happiness depends upon the consequences of the choices they make. A sacrifice now for a benefit later (such as higher education) is a choice that can have an important impact on the level of happiness, as can, consequently, the choice of a benefit now for a sacrifice later.

Perhaps happiness cannot be truly defined by comparing oneself to others as Bartram explained, surely there must be much more to it. If all people—immigrants, natives, and stayers—start to focus more on what they do have and less on what they do not, then an increase of happiness is sure to follow.

Critical Thinking

1. What are some of the road blocks in the pursuit of happiness?
2. Why does immigrating to a wealthier country result in lower economic status for new immigrants?

Create Central

www.mhhe.com/createcentral

Internet References

Statistical Modeling, Causal Inference, and Social Science
   http://andrewgelman.com/2006/11/27/immigration_and_1/
Migration Studies
   http://migration.oxfordjournals.org/content/1/2/156.full
Huffington Post
   http://www.huffingtonpost.com/2014/02/12/jon-stewart-gop-immigration_
n_4774026.html

Unit 2

UNIT

Prepared by: Sudip Ghosh, *Penn State University—Berks*

Microeconomics

Microeconomics primarily deals with individual behavior and firm behavior. How individuals optimize consumption and spending decisions given the budget constraint and how firms decide production decision given the cost constraint are core themes of microeconomics.

Microeconomics issues are main focus of this unit. Roots of modern microeconomics can be traced back to Adam Smith and *Wealth of Nations.* Adam Smith, who is also known as the father of modern economics, believed in free market capitalism and was a champion of laissez-faire ideology where role is rather limited in the whole process of allocation and pricing. According to him, an invisible hand drives the market.

With increased globalization, the competition has intensified and companies are forced to adopt strategies, which include the size of the target market, access to cheap and affordable resources, execution of innovative thoughts, and finally gaining access to newer territories.

Article   Prepared by: Sudip Ghosh, *Penn State University - Berks*

Who Lives Longest?—Healthy, Wealthy—and Famous

KENT SEPKOWITZ

Learning Outcomes

After reading this article, you will be able to:

• Recognize how obituaries can convey important economic messages to readers.

• See the social messages that obituaries convey.

The *New York Times* obituary section can tell us an awful lot. Using 999 consecutive obituaries that were published between 2009 and 2011, Australian researchers collected basic information on life span, occupation, cause of death, and gender of this famous bunch. And, perhaps not shockingly, the first detail they found was a large imbalance between the number of obituaries for men (813) and women (186), due no doubt to gender inequality as this group was coming of age.

Then there's the fact that famous men outlived famous women by about a year. Why? It's likely because famous women of that era were so often entertainers and athletes, the group in the study with the shortest life span, at 77 or 78 years. The authors found more cancer-related deaths among the performers and "creatives," including and especially deaths from lung cancer. In other words, those closest to the white-hot glare of the public spotlight—singers and dancers and athletes—fared the worst.

So who lived the longest? That honor goes to members of the military, who died at an average age of 85. It's a counterintuitive result, unless one keeps in mind that this study examines only the tiny few who reach the pinnacle of achievement. Next come the professionals and academics who died in their early 80s of, simply, "old age." They are followed by politicians who, on average, lived to be 82.

Although the small gradations in longevity among the famous are interesting, this study reveals a larger truth about health care: famous men in the study lived significantly longer—about four years—than "normal" men. There is a statistical quirk at play: many people who die young don't live long enough to become famous, overloading the "regular" side with younger deaths. This imbalance, however, can't fully explain the truth of the finding that, as the authors write, "wealth, recognition or related advantages" provide the famous a superior brand of health care. The study is thus grist for those who see good health care as a basic human right.

Critical Thinking

1. Explain the link between obituaries appearing in newspapers and one's social status.

2. How are fame and longevity related?

Create Central

www.mhhe.com/createcentral

Internet References

www.nhs.uk/news/2013/04April/Pages/No-evidence-that-price-of-fame-is-early-death.aspx

www.nytimes.com/2012/04/15/health/lester-breslow-who-tied-good-habits-to-longevity-dies-at-97.html?_r = 0

www.thedailybeast.com/newsweek/2013/04/29/who-lives-longest-the-surprising-health-benefits-of-fame.html

KENT SEPKOWITZ is an infectious-disease expert in New York City.

Article   Prepared by: Sudip Ghosh, *Penn State University—Berks*

Colorado in Jeopardy from Childhood Obesity Challenges

GABRIEL GUILLAUME

Learning Outcomes

After reading this article, you will be able to:

- Understand childhood obesity.

- Discuss the problems of childhood obesity.

"In March, the Colorado Health Foundation Report Card gave the health of Colorado's kids a C, and childhood obesity contributes strongly to this grade," writes Gabriel Guillaume. (Gregory Bull, *The Associated Press*)

A new childhood obesity study published in *JAMA Pediatrics*, a medical journal, found that national childhood obesity rates have increased in the past 14 years, contrary to a report released in February by the U.S. Centers for Disease Control and Prevention that reported a sharp decline in preschool obesity rates.

In March, the Colorado Health Foundation Report Card gave the health of Colorado's kids a C, and childhood obesity contributes strongly to this grade. Colorado is not immune to this larger national crisis and still has a long way to go in raising healthy kids.

We certainly need to celebrate the long-fought policy, capital improvements, and grassroots work that are helping to increase access to healthy food and physical activity here in Colorado.

Thanks to strategic investments by groups like the Colorado Health Foundation and Kaiser Permanente, schools are serving healthier fare, communities are building playgrounds and trails, organizations are funding grocery stores in low-income neighborhoods, and legislators are considering multiple bills that could affect childhood obesity.

However, we must remain vigilant on this issue in our state, where one in four children is overweight or obese, as is one in three Hispanic children. Our youngest kids are doing worse than our older children: 15 percent of children between the ages of 2 and 14

are obese, compared to 10 percent of our 10- to 17-year-olds. Kids who are obese as 5-year-olds are five times more likely to become obese adults. Rankings aside, these rates are far too high.

The healthy choice is often not the easy choice for many Colorado families. Colorado ranks 37th in the nation in the number of supermarkets per person, and one in five Colorado kids lives without access to affordable, healthy food. Increasing awareness of the importance of eating fresh fruits and vegetables daily does not work if a family does not have easy, affordable access to such produce.

Childhood obesity affects minority and low-income children at a higher level, and Colorado has the third fastest-rising rate of childhood poverty in the United States.

Also consider that only half of our children get the recommended amount of physical activity, and video games and television are not the only culprits. Colorado is one of the only four states that do not require school districts to set a minimum number of physical education classes or credits for students. Additionally, many low-income communities lack access to safe parks and playgrounds for activity after school and on weekends.

We need to act now as a state to make access to healthy eating and physical activity a priority for our future. Even seemingly small actions can have a tremendous impact.

As proof, several members in our LiveWell Moms network are making significant, inexpensive changes in their communities, whether by volunteering to manage the school snack program; shifting away from sweets-focused celebrations to instead provide fun, healthy options; or starting family physical activity programs in their neighborhoods.

Childhood obesity affects all of us. Medical costs for obesity-related disease are estimated at $1.64 billion in Colorado each year. What will it grow to when our children grow up?

We urge Coloradans not to be misled by our recent childhood obesity rankings and instead take stronger action than ever to foster change in their own homes, at school and in the community.

The only way we can turn the tide of childhood obesity entirely in Colorado is for everyone to take responsibility for making healthy choices available to all Coloradans, regardless of income or ZIP code.

Critical Thinking

1. What are specifically contributing to the childhood obesity problem in Colorado?
2. Are some rules discriminatory when it comes to childhood obesity?

Create Central

www.mhhe.com/createcentral

Internet References

Rocky Mountain PBS I-News
http://inewsnetwork.org/2013/03/21/childhood-obesity-rate-in-colorado-worrisome/

Let's Move!
http://www.letsmove.gov/health-problems-and-childhood-obesity

Family Education
http://life.familyeducation.com/obesity/social-isolation/61370.html

Article Prepared by: Sudip Ghosh, *Penn State University—Berks*

Price Tag for Childhood Obesity: $19,000 Per Kid

MICHELLE HEALY

Learning Outcomes

After reading this article, you will be able to:

- Discuss the financial costs of obesity.
- Understand the long-term financial and health effects of childhood obesity.

Over a lifetime, the medical costs associated with childhood obesity total about $19,000 per child compared with those for a child of normal weight, a new analysis shows.

The costs are about $12,900 per person for children of normal weight who become overweight or obese in adulthood, according to the analysis by researchers at the Duke Global Health Institute and Duke-NUS Graduate Medical School in Singapore and published online Monday in the journal *Pediatrics.*

The $19,000 estimate reflects direct medical costs such as doctors' visits and medication but not indirect costs such as absenteeism and lost productivity into adulthood. The cost is "large, although perhaps not as large as some people would have guessed," says lead author Eric Finkelstein, a health economist.

"In the case of childhood obesity, the real costs do not occur until decades later when these kids get adult health problems at a greater rate," he says.

Obesity is a known risk factor for cardiovascular disease, type 2 diabetes, certain cancers and a wide range of other diseases. About one in three adults and nearly one in five children in the United States are obese, according to the Centers for Disease Control and Prevention.

The estimates highlight "the financial consequences of inaction and the potential medical savings from obesity prevention efforts that successfully reduce or delay obesity onset," Finkelstein says.

The study notes that when multiplied by the number of all obese 10-year-olds in the U.S. today, the lifetime medical costs for this age alone reaches roughly $14 billion. That's nearly twice the Department of Health and Human Services' $7.8-billion budget for the Head Start program in fiscal year 2012, the analysis says.

To determine the estimates, researchers evaluated and updated existing research on lifetime costs of childhood obesity, focusing on six published studies.

The per-child estimates are valuable when looking at cost effectiveness, says John Cawley, co-director of the Institute on Health Economics, Health Behaviors and Disparities at Cornell University. He was not involved in the latest study.

If a new school-based intervention program is developed to decrease the probability of childhood obesity by a certain percentage, "you can use the numbers in the study to figure out what kind of savings that applies to the health care system," Cawley says.

The $19,000 estimate is more than roughly $16,930 the College Board says—one year of college costs at a public four-year institution, including tuition, fees, books, room and board and other expenses.

Critical Thinking

1. What challenges do obese kids face growing up?
2. How do we avoid childhood obesity?
3. What is the social cost of obesity among kids?

Create Central

www.mhhe.com/createcentral

Internet References

Pediatrics
   http://pediatrics.aappublications.org/content/early/2014/04/02/peds.2014-0063.abstract

Medical News Toda
   http://www.medicalnewstoday.com/articles/275109.php
Time
   http://time.com/50986/this-is-how-much-childhood-obesity-costs-over-a-lifetime/

Article   Prepared by: Sudip Ghosh, *Penn State University—Berks*

Why Colorado and Washington Were Wise to Legalize Pot

Scott Shane

Learning Outcomes

After reading this article, you will be able to:

- Define entrepreneurship.

- Define recreational marijuana.

- Discuss varying attitudes toward marijuana use.

Like water finding a path, entrepreneurs will always figure out a way to respond to business opportunities. That's why other states should follow the example of Colorado and Washington and legalize the recreational use of marijuana. Harnessing the power of entrepreneurs is much more productive than fighting it.

On January 1, Colorado legalized the sale of small amounts of marijuana for recreational use. Later this year, Washington will follow suit. Alaska, Arizona, California, D.C., and Oregon may be the next states to permit cannabis businesses.

Cultural attitudes, fairness, economics, and entrepreneurial behavior all point to extension of this trend toward legalization. Much like policy makers were caught flat-footed as American attitudes toward same-sex marriage changed, so too have they missed the shifting views toward the legalization of pot. According to an October 2013 Gallup Organization poll, 58 percent of Americans now favor legalization of marijuana—a jump of 10 percentage points over the previous year. Many policymakers seem to have missed the memo showing that voters' views on the topic are fundamentally different from the late 1960s, when only one-in-nine Americans favored sanctioning it.

Fairness, too, justifies legalizing cannabis. In the 48 states that do not permit recreational use of marijuana, smoking tobacco, which causes cancer, is legal. By contrast, smoking weed, which

is used to treat the symptoms of cancer treatments, is not. Moreover, some experts believe that alcohol, which is legal in virtually all parts of the United States, is more harmful than marijuana, which is illegal in almost all of the country.

Fairness dictates that policymakers either need to play nanny and ban everything that's bad for us—from sugar-laden soda to fat-filled fast food—or they need to allow Americans to make adult decisions about what they want to put in their bodies. Making cigarettes, beer, and whiskey legal, while banning joints and hash brownies, unfairly favors the makers of certain harmful products.

Making pot legal has economic benefits. Policymakers can tax sales of the product—and are doing so relatively heavily. Both Washington and Colorado are charging a 25 percent tax on pot sales, with even higher rates in some municipalities. The non-partisan Tax Foundation estimates that Colorado will bring in nearly $70 million in new taxes, with initial proceeds being used for school construction. Because tax revenues are expected to exceed school building needs, Colorado public officials are already thinking of additional ways to use the tax windfall.

By making pot legal, police can focus their attention on stopping more destructive illegal drugs like cocaine and heroin, which are more likely to cause crime and health problems. That would help financially strapped states. If all states legalized cannabis sales, the reduced drug enforcement costs and higher tax revenues would be worth more than $17 billion to them, a 2010 Cato Institute study revealed.

Legalized pot will also produce public health benefits, Forbes reports. Because alcohol consumption is more harmful to people than marijuana use, but the two are substitutes, legalizing pot will lead customers to shift to the better of the two choices.

Entrepreneurs find and pursue market opportunities wherever they are. Making a business illegal doesn't get rid of the efforts of entrepreneurs to pursue it. Everyone knows that entrepreneurs are selling marijuana for recreational use in all 48 states where it is illegal.

Making a business legal makes it easier for policymakers to tap entrepreneurial efforts to benefit society. Colorado and Washington are using taxes and regulation to channel pot entrepreneurship more productively than other states, where policy makers are wasting resources trying to stop it, and, consequently, driving it underground.

Critical Thinking

1. Why are Colorado and Washington State taking the lead on legalizing recreational marijuana?
2. What are the advantages of legalizing marijuana on the society?
3. Illustrate what happens if pot remains illegal in the US.

Create Central

www.mhhe.com/createcentral

Internet References

Business Insider
   http://www.businessinsider.com/weedmaps-justin-hartfield-entrepreneur-marijuana-legalization-2013-4
Culture and Entrepreneurship
   http://theculturalentrepreneur.wordpress.com/2013/07/26/marijuana-opportunity-and-entrepreneurship/
Market Watch
   http://www.marketwatch.com/story/marijuana-entrepreneur-jamen-shively-discusses-plandai-biotechnology-branding-cannabis-and-legalization-2014-02-04

Shane, Scott. From *Entrepreneur.com*, January 20, 2014. Copyright © 2014 Entrepreneur. Reprinted with permission.

Unit 3

UNIT

Prepared by: Sudip Ghosh, *Penn State University — Berks*

The Economics of Work and Income

Economic fairness is not without serious criticism. Advocates of fairness believe in an equal society, while they maintain that such a system is inherently weak; since people differ in their natural abilities, and they come from different socioeconomic backgrounds, they believe that helping people is valuable, but not free. The more you help low-income people, the more low-income people you'll have. The more you help unemployed people, the more unemployed people you'll have which will have a perverse effect on the economy. However, there is widespread disagreement within the economics profession on two questions. First, if inequality is to serve as an incentive to great efficiency, exactly how unequal should the income distribution be? Secondly, what role should the government play to ensure equality.

Differences in the distribution of wealth have been even greater over the last decade. In 2007, the bottom 40 percent of the U.S. population essentially had zero wealth, while the top fifth accounted for 85 percent of all the American wealth. While most Americans are better-off today (in terms of the absolute amount of income and wealth available) than they might have been, say, 50 years ago, certain trends have been disturbing. To address these issues this unit focuses on gender wage discrimination, raising state minimum wages, retraining and retaining trained workers, and means for government to fund these programs by legalizing and taxing marijuana.

Article   Prepared by: Sudip Ghosh, *Penn State University—Berks*

Freezing Paradise: an Update on Global Gender Equality

MICHAEL AIKEN

Learning Outcomes

After reading this article, you will be able to:

- Understand more about gender equality.

- Understand and define the wage gap.

- Discuss how indices measure economic opportunity for males and females.

Northern Europe may have a cold climate, but for many women it is paradise nonetheless. In matters of gender equality, Nordic countries lead the way, according to the 2013 Global Gender Gap Report, issued by the World Economic Forum (WEF).

The rankings are derived from an indexed calculation of male-female ratios of these categories:

- Economic Opportunity: labor force participation, income equality, and career advancement
- Educational Attainment: female access to education and literacy rate
- Health and Survival: life expectancy and sex ratio (measures societal preference for sons)
- Political Empowerment: females holding political office or ministerial positions

Iceland, Finland, Norway, and Sweden remained the four highest ranked countries in the overall index, while Denmark trailed close behind at number eight. European countries dominated the top 25—high performers included Ireland, Switzerland, Belgium, Germany, Latvia, the Netherlands, and the United Kingdom. From the Asia-Pacific region, the Philippines and New Zealand cracked the top 10—fifth and seventh,

respectively. Australia, Canada, Cuba, Lesotho, Nicaragua, South Africa, and the United States also were among the top 25 performers.

The 136 countries in the index (representing 90 percent of the world's population) have made progress in closing the health/survival and education attainment gender gaps—96 and 93 percent, respectively. However, gaps in economic opportunity and political empowerment persist. According to the WEF report, only 60 percent of the economic outcomes gap has been closed, while progress toward closing the political outcomes gap remains at 21 percent.

Overall, global trends indicate a slow, but steady shift toward gender equality. Eighty-six percent of the 110 countries evaluated since 2006 have demonstrated improved performance over the last four years, whereas only 15 countries have shown widening gender gaps. The most improved countries since 2006 include Switzerland, Nicaragua, Bolivia, Ecuador, Saudi Arabia, Cameroon, and Yemen; countries that lost ground include Mali, Jordan, Kuwait, and Zambia—all in the bottom quartile.

On the economic and political fronts, Iceland, Finland, Norway, and Sweden are the definitive leaders in closing the gender gap. These Nordic countries enjoy the highest labor force participation rates for women and have the smallest salary gaps between men and women; additionally, women enjoy greater opportunities to hold political and economic leadership positions. Countries like the United States, Canada, and the United Kingdom ranked lower on the overall index due to the economic and political gender gaps that persist.

Progress toward gender equality in Nordic countries stems from the socio-economic policies that allow for greater female participation in the workforce—including mandatory parental leave, maternity leave, and parental leave benefits funded by social insurance funds and employers. Additionally, post-maternity re-entry programs allow women greater ease in continuing to work post pregnancy. Countries that employ the talents, ideas, and leadership of educated women in the workforce are more likely to enjoy greater economic productivity and technological innovation.

Compared to their southern neighbors, Nordic countries will be prepared to handle the economic pressures of aging population due to greater female participation in the workforce. Female-friendly policies here already have led to higher fertility rates and greater economic participation as compared to other OECD countries. Nordic countries have fertility rates between 1.88 and 1.67, as compared to countries like South Korea, Japan, Germany, Austria, Italy, and Spain—with rates in the 1.4 range and as low as 1.24 (South Korea). Canada, the United Kingdom, and the United States each have birthrates around the replacement rate, which ensures a stable population. Given a replacement rate of 2.1, 0.3 can make a big difference in a country's economic future, and the Nordic countries have the clear advantage in this respect as compared to the rest of Europe.

Unlike the Nordic leaders, some states that have made investments in women's education—including Japan, the United Arab Emirates, and Brazil—may fail to utilize the talents of its educated women, thereby missing out on much-needed economic growth. In the Middle East, where investment has reduced the education gap between men and women, countries have failed to reduce the gap in economic participation, leading to a similar result. Though no country has achieved complete gender parity, falling fertility rates and the widespread focus on economic growth in the developed world fall may prompt further progress. Predictably, gender equality in developing countries likely will take longer to achieve, though steady progress is expected to continue.

Critical Thinking

1. What is the global trend in gender equality?
2. How are developed nations ranked compared to third-world countries? Why?
3. Why isn't investment in women's education fully tapped?

Create Central

www.mhhe.com/createcentral

Internet References

Institute for Women's Policy Research
http://www.iwpr.org/initiatives/pay-equity-and-discrimination

Huffington Post
http://www.huffingtonpost.com/soraya-chemaly/wage-equality_b_1415560.html

National Committee on Pay Equity
http://www.pay-equity.org/

Forbes
http://www.forbes.com/sites/peggydrexler/2014/04/10/equal-pay-for-equal-work-seems-like-a-no-brainer-right/

Aiken, Michael. From *Diplomatic Courier*, May 10, 2014. Copyright © 2014 Diplomatic Courier. Reprinted with permission.

Article

Prepared by: Sudip Ghosh, *Penn State University—Berks*

There's a Fly in My Soup: Can Insects Satisfy World Food Needs?

How the real caveman diet will help meet our global food needs.

Stewart M. Patrick

Learning Outcomes

After reading this article, you will be able to:

- Understand the importance of bugs in our food chain.
- Describe how bug eating will let poor people have access to easy protein meals.

What world traveler hasn't declined at least one local "delicacy"? A decade ago in Oaxaca, Mexico, I turned up my nose at chapulines, a steaming plate of toasted grasshoppers. "Tastes like chicken," my waiter said as he smiled unconvincingly. But overcoming disgust for "edible insects" may be the easiest way to meet global food needs, according to a fascinating, if occasionally stomach-churning, report from the UN's Food and Agricultural Agency (FAO), which is based, of all places, in Rome.

> **In the future, one could imagine trendsetters like Anthony Bordain competing with counterparts to see who can make the tastiest dragonfly confit.**

The notion of meeting caloric, especially protein, needs from insects (as well as grubs, worms and other creepy-crawlies) is hardly new. It's something humans and their hominid ancestors have been doing for millions of years. Paleoanthropologists and biologists speculate that our Paleolithic ancestors consumed prodigious quantities of insects—a fact conveniently omitted by most contempoary aficionados of the "cave man diet." More recently, 19th century European arrivals to Australia marveled at aboriginal tribes' insatiable appetite for insects and the dramatic impact such a diet could have on their health and appearance, as documented in a fascinating ethnography, *The Moth Hunters.*

What's surprising is how enduring the human taste for Insecta remains. According to the FAO, more than two billion people—30 percent of humanity—already supplement their diet with insects. And given the number of insects out there—*1 million distinct species* have already been identified and nearly 2,000 proven edible—diners have a crunchy smorgasbord to choose from. "The most commonly eaten insect groups," we learn, "are beetles, caterpillars, bees, wasps, ants, grasshoppers, locusts, crickets, cicadas, leaf and planthoppers, scale insects and true bugs, termites, dragonflies and flies."

Most of today's insect-eaters live in the developing world, in countries where insects are perceived as a perfectly acceptable and convenient source of energy: readily (or at least seasonally) available, highly portable, and requiring fewer inputs than agriculture or animal husbandry. In terms of nutrition, insects provide outstanding advantages, having "high fat, protein, fiber, vitamin, and mineral content," and can be a particularly important diet component for children under the age of five in poor countries.

While many in the West may recoil in disgust, the FAO makes a compelling case on food security grounds for entomophagy (eating bugs, in science-speak). Often dismissed as "famine foods," insects may offer at least part of the answer to the global food crisis. And a crisis is what we have on our hands. Based on current demographic and dietary trends, as I've written before, the world needs to double its food production over the next 40 years—an effort that will require unprecedented productivity gains while risking ecological calamity.

Here's where bugs come in. Insects, it turns out, are far more efficient than livestock—perhaps 10 times so—in transforming feed into edible meat. And they largely avoid the huge greenhouse gas emissions, as well as other environmental pollutants, associated with cows and pigs. While most edible insects continue to be collected in the wild, more organized forms of insect farming have emerged, including "cricket farming" in Laos, Thailand, and Vietnam. Insects are also being increasingly used as animal feed, particularly for poultry and accquaculture. By providing employment opportunities, the edible insect sector has a potential role to play in rural development, from Southeast Asia to Central Africa.

To have a real impact on food consumption patterns, however, edible insects must go global. Today, the international trade in these commodities is neglible, limited to niche markets like fulfilling the dietary desires of diaspora populations.

Expanding global trade in edible insects will require expanding existing national and multilateral health and sanitary regulations. This will include updating the *Codex Alimentarius*, created by FAO and the World Health Organization in 1963 to harmonize international food standards and codes of practice.

The biggest stumbling block to expanding global consumption of insects is cultural. The very idea of eating bugs remains taboo in many countries, particularly in the wealthy West, where they tend to be confined to "novelty snacks." There may be ways to make inroads against this stigma, however. A few celebrity U.S. chefs have put insect items on their restaurant menus. In the future, one could imagine trend-setters like Anthony Bordain competing with counterparts to see who can make the tastiest dragonfly confit. Who knows? With Manhattan and L.A. foodies leading the charge, would Middle America be far behind?

So, if you're inclined to take one for global food security, or just want to set the trend in your hometown, you're in luck. Since 2010, the FAO has created a useful *"Webportal of Edible Insects,"* listing your culinary options. Be sure to check out the chapulines. I hear they taste like chicken.

Critical Thinking

1. Explain what happens when bug consumption becomes a vogue.
2. How is eating bugs good for the environment?
3. In what ways does bug eating address issues of malnutrition?

Create Central

www.mhhe.com/createcentral

Internet References

www.un.org/apps/news/story.asp?newsid=25662&cr=insects#.Uc3eXFL7dM4

http://qz.com/84127/five-reasons-we-should-all-be-eating-insects

www.commonsensehome.com/eating-bugs

http://redicecreations.com/article.php?id=25106

http://inhabitat.com/un-report-says-we-should-be-eating-more-bugs

Article

Prepared by: Sudip Ghosh, *Penn State University—Berks*

Shortchanged

Statistics show that women get paid less than men for equal work. So why is it still so hard for them to prove it?

PETER COY AND ELIZABETH DWOSKIN

Learning Outcomes

After reading this article, you will be able to:

- Relate to gender discrimination that still exists in the U.S. salary structure.

- Discover ways to make pay equal for similar responsibility despite gender differences.

Lilly Ledbetter discovered she was underpaid one spring evening in 1998 at the start of her overnight shift as a manager at the Goodyear Tire & Rubber plant in Gadsden, Ala. She checked her mailbox as usual and found an anonymous note. On it was scribbled her monthly pay along with the pay of three men who started the same year she did and had the same job. The men were earning 15 to 40 percent more. "My heart jerked as if an electric jolt had coursed through my body," she wrote in her 2012 memoir, *Grace and Grit: My Fight for Equal Pay and Fairness at Goodyear and Beyond.* Ledbetter had worked at Goodyear for 19 years but was never quite sure she was being paid unfairly. "I was like a wife nursing a nagging suspicion that her husband's having an affair."

Pay discrimination is a silent offense. Women know when they're being harassed and abused, of course, and they can often tell if they're being discriminated against in hiring and promotion—all they have to do is count the men with lesser skills and credentials doing jobs they still aspire to. But in many workplaces, discussing pay is frowned upon; in some, it's a dismissible offense. So, like Ledbetter, women often don't know when they're getting paid less than men. So they don't complain. So the problem continues.

President Kennedy promised America would put a man on the moon and would stop pay discrimination against women. One of those happened. The Equal Pay Act that Kennedy signed in 1963 prohibited "discrimination on account of sex in the payment of wages by employers engaged in commerce or in the production of goods for commerce." Yet nearly half a century

later, in the first three months of 2012, women still earned only 82.2 percent of what men earned. That's comparing the "usual median weekly earnings" of full-time employees. Comparing annual pay of full-time, year-round workers, women earned only 77 percent of what men earned in 2010.

The latest hope for closing the gap died on June 5, when Senate Republicans filibustered a bill to make it easier for employees to share information about their pay. Three days later a federal judge in San Francisco said he was "seriously concerned" that lawyers for 45,000 female employees of Wal-Mart Stores in California haven't shown enough evidence to file a sex-discrimination class action. There has been progress toward gender parity since Kennedy's day, but for many women, not enough.

The gender pay gap, around 40¢ to the dollar in the early 1960s, shrank rapidly in the 1980s and early '90s. It has narrowed by only 4¢ since 1994 and less than 1¢ since 2005, even though younger women have caught up to and surpassed men in education. What's more, pay difference actually grows as a woman's career progresses, adding up to hundreds of thousands of dollars on average over a lifetime. Catherine Hill, head of research at the American Association of University Women, found that among college graduates, the pay gap grew from 20¢ on the dollar one year after graduation to 31¢ by the 10th reunion.

Only some of the pay gap is the result of discrimination by employers. Men crowd into high-paying fields like engineering, while women dominate lower-paying fields like education and social service. And women are more likely than men to fall off the career track when they have children. They take time off and lose skills, or they opt for less-demanding jobs so they can spend more time at home. Most fathers, in contrast, manage to skate through parenthood without the slightest harm to their careers. Employers could offer family-friendlier policies on leave and flextime, but they can't be blamed for dads who don't do enough around the house.

In a 2009 report commissioned by the Department of Labor, Consad Research of Pittsburgh concluded that all but 5¢ to 7¢

Mind the Pay Gap
Women's pay as a percentage of men's in 2010

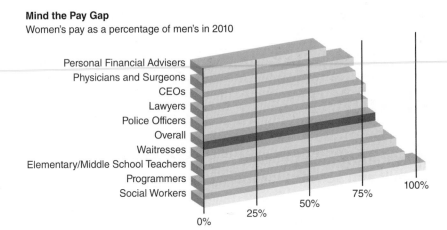

Personal Financial Advisers
Physicians and Surgeons
CEOs
Lawyers
Police Officers
Overall
Waitresses
Elementary/Middle School Teachers
Programmers
Social Workers

0% 25% 50% 75% 100%

of the wage gap could be explained by factors other than outright discrimination. "It is not possible now, and doubtless will never be possible, to determine reliably whether any portion of the observed gender wage gap . . . can confidently be attributed to overt discrimination against women," the contractors wrote.

However, other researchers do detect gender bias. In a 2007 article for the Academy of Management's journal *Perspectives,* Cornell University labor economists Francine Blau and Lawrence Kahn wrote that even after adjusting for education, experience, race, industry, and occupation, women brought home just 91 percent of what men did. And they said that figure may understate the pay gap due to sex discrimination if women have been excluded from higher-paying opportunities. "There is evidence that although discrimination against women in the labor market has declined, some discrimination does still continue to exist," they wrote.

Lilly Ledbetter didn't need dueling statistical analyses to tell her she was underpaid once she saw how much male managers at the tire plant were getting. Winning a judgment was the problem. A jury found it was "more likely than not" that she suffered pay discrimination, but the Supreme Court turned her down on appeal because she didn't complain within 180 days of when she was first underpaid. The Lilly Ledbetter Fair Pay Restoration Act, the first law President Obama signed upon taking office in 2009, fixed that for future plaintiffs by treating each undersized paycheck as a fresh, punishable offense.

The bigger problem remains: If there's no tipster stuffing notes in their mailboxes, women don't know they're underpaid. The Paycheck Fairness Act, which passed in the House in 2009, would fix that deficiency by preventing companies from retaliating against workers who inquire about pay gaps. It would also allow for punitive damages; close some loopholes that employers have used to justify pay gaps; and require employers to submit salary data that would make it easier to detect violations. The Senate GOP's June 5 filibuster of the bill played into the hands of Democrats seeking women's votes, as did defensive quotes from Republican senators. Marco Rubio of Florida said he didn't think the bill would accomplish its purpose, and "reads more to me like some sort of welfare plan for trial lawyers." (Wisconsin passed a similar law in 2009 and saw no boom in litigation, according to its Department of Workforce Development.)

A lack of good data impedes progress on fair pay. Nationwide statistics can't prove that any particular woman has been treated unfairly, while individual cases are too idiosyncratic—an employer can usually cite some justification for why she got less than the guy in the next cubicle. For potential plaintiffs, the ideal would be to have reams of detailed data about every company's pay by gender, job title, and so on. But that would be a paperwork nightmare, and few companies would willingly expose themselves that way.

By grouping employees in different ways, expert witnesses in lawsuits brought against Boeing, Wal-Mart, and Novartis have drawn opposite conclusions about whether discrimination exists. In 2006 the Bush administration discontinued a program started by the Clinton administration to collect data from federal contractors (who account for 25 percent of the civilian workforce) on the grounds that the data weren't useful. The Obama administration is looking into restarting data collection for contractors to detect patterns of discrimination but still faces opposition from employer groups. "Will the usefulness justify the burden?" asks Rebecca Springer, an attorney at Crowell & Moring, a law firm that represents defendants in Equal Pay Act lawsuits.

Fair question. And yet solutions exist. Labor economist Marc Bendick Jr. argues that fears about excessive paperwork are overblown: Just a small amount of easy-to-supply data would be enough, he says, to flag companies that bear further investigation. Employers' attorney William Doyle Jr. of Morgan, Lewis & Bockius would encourage employers to investigate their own practices by promising that their findings could not be used against them in court. Both ideas have merit. Doing nothing amounts to preserving a code of silence that continues to hurt women. Just ask Ledbetter, now 74, who never got a settlement from Goodyear and recently had to scrape money together to replace a busted air conditioner. "Trust me," she says, "I have learned how behind women and their families are, and it's getting this nation dragged down."

Critical Thinking

1. Why does a glass ceiling still exist in the U.S. pay structure?
2. Explain the social reaction to gender-based pay discrimination.
3. Explain how such challenges are addressed in America.

Create Central

www.mhhe.com/createcentral

Internet References

www.payscale.com/career-news/2009/11/women-earn-less-than-men-a-result-of-pregnancy-leave

www.huffingtonpost.com/2013/05/30/payscale-study-women_n_3360863.html

http://economix.blogs.nytimes.com/2009/11/16/the-gender-pay-gap-persists-especially-for-the-rich/?_r=0

www.businessweek.com/articles/2012-10-25/why-women-earn-less-than-men-a-year-out-of-school

Article   Prepared by: Sudip Ghosh, *Penn State University—Berks*

Gender Pay and Leadership Gaps Are Real—and Impact Our Economy

ILENE H. LANG

Learning Outcomes

After reading this article, you will be able to:

- Relate to gender discrimination that still exists in the U.S. salary structure.

- Find why the gender pay gap is still a reality 160 years after the Seneca Falls, NY, summit produced the "Declaration of Sentiments."

G enerations have passed since America's first women's summit produced the Declaration of Sentiments at Seneca Falls, New York. This document listed an array of "injuries and usurpations" directed toward women, chiefly: "He has monopolized nearly all the profitable employments, and from those she is permitted to follow, she receives but a scanty remuneration."

Yet more than 160 years after Seneca Falls, women still lag men in pay and business leadership positions in the United States. In testimony this week at a Joint Economic Committee hearing on the gender pay gap, I outlined the current landscape of workplace inequity.

It isn't pretty.

Catalyst's report, Pipeline's Broken Promise, surveyed more than 4,100 women and men M.B.A. alumni from 26 top business schools worldwide—including 12 from leading U.S. universities. We discovered that women averaged $4,600 less in their initial jobs out of business school, even after controlling for job level, years of pre-M.B.A. work experience, industry, region, and time since earning the M.B.A.

Catalyst found that women started at lower levels than men after controlling for career aspirations and parenthood status. And women were outpaced by men in salary throughout their careers—regardless of whether or not they had kids. This gap in pay only intensified as time went on.

If our "best and brightest" women face these challenges, can you imagine what's happening throughout the rest of the system? A look at women leadership in America's top companies and the picture darkens.

For more than a decade, Catalyst has meticulously counted the number of women in leadership in Fortune 500 companies. The Fortune 500 is important because the country's most powerful and influential companies set the standard. While women are currently 46.4 percent of total Fortune 500 employees, they are only 13.5 percent of Executive Officers, hold 15.2 percent of board seats, and are just 2.6 percent of CEOs. That means that of 500 CEOs, only 13 are women and 487 are men.

The recently released Government Accountability Office (GAO) report on the pay gap for women in management—also unveiled at this week's Joint Economic Committee hearing—found that female managers earn just 81 cents for every dollar male managers are making. The report also described a leadership gap that cuts across industries. One might expect female-prevalent industries like retail or finance would have high representations of women in leadership—but they do not. This is despite the fact that women have been outpacing men with Bachelor's and Master's degrees since the 1980s.

The Catalyst Census of F500 companies and the new GAO report reveal the extent to which our nation's top companies are not meritocracies. When an organization values women and men equally, the gender balance should be the same at all levels—top and bottom. When it's not, ingrained biases are halting progress for half of the talent pool.

Catalyst research reveals how a "think-leader-think-male" mindset dominates talent management systems in corporate America. Traits and behaviors that organizations seek in their future leadership pipeline are too often modeled on current incumbents who are overwhelmingly male. And women are still penalized for behaving in ways that men are rewarded for. I call this the Goldilocks syndrome: "Too tough, too soft, but never just right."

Why should we care? Because promoting women to leadership and paying them equitably is not only the right thing to do. It's the smart thing to do.

When a woman's career is stifled, family income takes a hit. That's less money for essentials like food, clothing, and doctor's visits—let alone things like flat-screen TVs, SUVs, and trips to Disneyland. The ripple effect on our economy is enormous.

Furthermore, Catalyst's Bottom Line research found that Fortune 500 companies with more women corporate officers, on average, financially outperformed those with fewer. The same holds true when more women are in the boardroom. On average, companies with more women on their corporate boards outperform those with fewer by 53 percent on Return on Equity, 42 percent on Return on Sales, and 66 percent on Return on Invested Capital. Shareholders look twice at this kind of performance!

Our research also shows that women aspire to success just as much as men do, and they define it similarly. But women are still paid less and are forced to navigate a corporate culture that holds women to different standards and makes it tougher for them to succeed.

To break down these barriers, Catalyst advises companies to root out unintended stereotyping and establish strict accountability regarding promotion and compensation equity. "Sunlight is said to be the best of disinfectants," wrote Louis Brandeis. When it comes to exposing pay inequity, I couldn't agree more.

Sunlight is starting to hit public companies and mutual funds. A new U.S. Securities and Exchange Commission (SEC) rule mandates that they must disclose in their proxy statements whether or not diversity is a consideration when directors are named. If these companies consider diversity during appointment proceedings, the SEC requires disclosure of how this policy is implemented, and how the board (or nominating committees) evaluates the effectiveness of this diversity policy.

This federal response is an important first step. Another bold move forward would be for the Senate to join the House in passing the Paycheck Fairness Act. This law mandates, among other things, increased transparency on compensation.

Too much is at stake to ignore the problem of gender inequity. Our economic health will continue to take a hit as long as "injuries and usurpations" of pay and promotions—in the words of 19th century trailblazers—persist.

Critical Thinking

1. Why does the glass ceiling still exist in the U.S. pay structure?

2. Explain the social reaction to gender-based pay discrimination.

3. How are such challenges addressed in the United States?

Create Central

www.mhhe.com/createcentral

Internet References

www.payscale.com/career-news/2009/11/women-earn-less-than -men-a-result-of-pregnancy-leave

www.huffingtonpost.com/2013/05/30/payscale-study-women _n_3360863.html

http://economix.blogs.nytimes.com/2009/11/16/the-gender-pay-gap -persists-especially-for-the-rich/?_r=0

www.businessweek.com/articles/2012-10-25/why-women-earn-less -than-men-a-year-out-of-school

ILENE H. LANG is president and chief executive officer of Catalyst. Founded in 1962, Catalyst is the leading nonprofit working globally to advance women and business.

Article   Prepared by: Sudip Ghosh, *Penn State University—Berks*

The Effect of Immigrants on U.S. Employment and Productivity

GIOVANNI PERI

Learning Outcomes

After reading this article, you will be able to:

• Understand the dynamism of the U.S. economy and how it shed and added jobs each month.

• Determine if the new immigrant labor supply displaced U.S.-born workers.

• Explain how net immigrants expand the U.S. economy's productive capacity.

The effects of immigration on the total output and income of the U.S. economy can be studied by comparing output per worker and employment in states that have had large immigrant inflows with data from states that have few new foreign-born workers. Statistical analysis of state-level data shows that immigrants expand the economy's productive capacity by stimulating investment and promoting specialization. This produces efficiency gains and boosts income per worker. At the same time, evidence is scant that immigrants diminish the employment opportunities of U.S.-born workers.

Immigration in recent decades has significantly increased the presence of foreign-born workers in the United States. The impact of these immigrants on the U.S. economy is hotly debated. Some stories in the popular press suggest that immigrants diminish the job opportunities of workers born in the United States. Others portray immigrants as filling essential jobs that are shunned by other workers. Economists who have analyzed local labor markets have mostly failed to find large effects of immigrants on employment and wages of U.S.-born workers (see Borjas 2006; Card 2001, 2007, 2009; and Card and Lewis 2007).

This *Economic Letter* summarizes recent research by Peri (2009) and Peri and Sparber (2009) examining the impact of immigrants on the broader U.S. economy. These studies systematically analyze how immigrants affect total output, income per worker, and employment in the short and long run. Consistent with previous research, the analysis finds no significant effect of immigration on net job growth for U.S.-born workers in these time horizons. This suggests that the economy absorbs immigrants by expanding job opportunities rather than by displacing workers born in the United States. Second, at the state level, the presence of immigrants is associated with increased output per worker. This effect emerges in the medium to long run as businesses adjust their physical capital, that is, equipment and structures, to take advantage of the labor supplied by new immigrants. However, in the short run, when businesses have not fully adjusted their productive capacity, immigrants reduce the capital intensity of the economy. Finally, immigration is associated with an increase in average hours per worker and a reduction in skills per worker as measured by the share of college-educated workers in a state. These two effects have opposite and roughly equal effect on labor productivity.

The Method

A major challenge to immigration research is the difficulty of identifying the effects of immigration on economic variables when we do not observe what would have happened if immigration levels had been different, all else being equal. To get around this problem, we take advantage of the fact that the increase in immigrants has been very uneven across states. For example, in California, one worker in three was foreign born in 2008, while in West Virginia the comparable proportion was only one in 100. By exploiting variations in the inflows of immigrants across states at 10-year intervals from 1960 to 2000, and annually from 1994 to 2008, we are able to estimate the short-run (one to two years), medium-run (four years), and long-run (seven to ten years) impact of immigrants on output, income, and employment.

To ensure that we are isolating the effects of immigrants rather than effects of other factors, we control for a range of variables

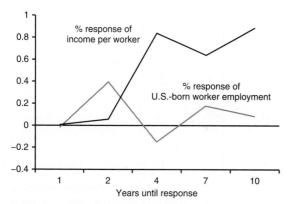

Figure 1   Employment and income

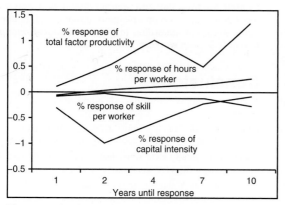

Figure 2   Capital intensity, hours per worker, and total factor productivity

that might contribute to differences in economic outcomes. These include sector specialization, research spending, openness to trade, technology adoption, and others. We then compare economic outcomes in states that experienced increases in immigrant inflows with states that did not experience significant increases.

As a further control for isolating the specific effects of immigration, we focus on variations in the flow of immigrants that are caused by geographical and historical factors and are not the result of state-specific economic conditions. For example, a state may experience rapid growth, which attracts a lot of immigrants and also affects output, income, and employment. In terms of geography, proximity to the Mexican border is associated with high net immigration because border states tend to get more immigrants. Historical migration patterns also are a factor because immigrants are drawn to areas with established immigrant communities. These geography and history-driven flows increase the presence of immigrants, but do not reflect state-specific economic conditions. Hence, economic outcomes associated with these flows are purer measures of the impact of immigrants on economic variables.

The Short- and the Long-run Effects of Immigrants

Immigration effects on employment, income, and productivity vary by occupation, job, and industry. Nonetheless, it is possible to total these effects to get an aggregate economic impact. Here we attempt to quantify the aggregate gains and losses for the U.S. economy from immigration. If the average impact on employment and income per worker is positive, this implies an aggregate "surplus" from immigration. In other words, the total gains accruing to some U.S.-born workers are larger than the total losses suffered by others.

Figures 1 and 2 show the response of key economic variables to an inflow of immigrants equal to 1% of employment. Figure 1 shows the impact on employment of U.S.-born workers and on average income per worker after one, two, four, seven, and ten years. Figure 2 shows the impact on the components of income per worker: physical capital intensity, as measured by capital per unit of output; skill intensity, as measured by human capital per worker; average hours worked; and total factor productivity, measuring productive efficiency and technological level. Some interesting patterns emerge.

First, there is no evidence that immigrants crowd out U.S.-born workers in either the short or long run. Data on U.S.-born worker employment imply small effects, with estimates never statistically different from zero. The impact on hours per worker is similar. We observe insignificant effects in the short run and a small but significant positive effect in the long run. At the same time, immigration reduces somewhat the skill intensity of workers in the short and long run because immigrants have a slightly lower average education level than U.S.-born workers.

Second, the positive long-run effect on income per U.S.-born worker accrues over some time. In the short run, small insignificant effects are observed. Over the long run, however, a net inflow of immigrants equal to 1% of employment increases income per worker by 0.6% to 0.9%. This implies that total immigration to the United States from 1990 to 2007 was associated with a 6.6% to 9.9% increase in real income per worker. That equals an increase of about $5,100 in the yearly income of the average U.S. worker in constant 2005 dollars. Such a gain equals 20% to 25% of the total real increase in average yearly income per worker registered in the United States between 1990 and 2007.

The third result is that the long-run increase in income per worker associated with immigrants is mainly due to increases in the efficiency and productivity of state economies. This effect becomes apparent in the medium to long run. Such a gradual response of productivity is accompanied by a gradual response of capital intensity. While in the short run, physical capital per unit of output is decreased by net immigration, in the medium to long run, businesses expand their equipment and physical plant proportionally to their increase in production.

How Can These Patterns Be Explained?

The effects identified above can be explained by adjustments businesses make over time that allow them to take full advantage of the new immigrant labor supply. These adjustments, including upgrading and expanding capital stock, provide businesses with opportunities to expand in response to hiring immigrants.

This process can be analyzed at the state level (see Peri and Sparber 2009). The analysis begins with the well-documented phenomenon that U.S.-born workers and immigrants tend to take different occupations. Among less-educated workers, those born in the United States tend to have jobs in manufacturing or mining, while immigrants tend to have jobs in personal services and agriculture. Among more-educated workers, those born in the United States tend to work as managers, teachers, and nurses, while immigrants tend to work as engineers, scientists, and doctors. Second, within industries and specific businesses, immigrants and U.S.-born workers tend to specialize in different job tasks. Because those born in the United States have relatively better English language skills, they tend to specialize in communication tasks. Immigrants tend to specialize in other tasks, such as manual labor. Just as in the standard concept of comparative advantage, this results in specialization and improved production efficiency.

If these patterns are driving the differences across states, then in states where immigration has been heavy, U.S.-born workers with less education should have shifted toward more communication-intensive jobs. Figure 3 shows exactly this. The share of immigrants among the less educated is strongly correlated with the extent of U.S.-born worker specialization in communication tasks. Each point in the graph represents a U.S. state in 2005. In states with a heavy concentration of less-educated immigrants, U.S.-born workers have migrated toward more communication-intensive occupations. Those jobs pay higher wages than manual jobs, so such a mechanism has stimulated the productivity of workers born in the United States and generated new employment opportunities.

To better understand this mechanism, it is useful to consider the following hypothetical illustration. As young immigrants with low schooling levels take manually intensive construction jobs, the construction companies that employ them have opportunities to expand. This increases the demand for construction supervisors, coordinators, designers, and so on. Those are occupations with greater communication intensity and are typically staffed by U.S.-born workers who have moved away from manual construction jobs. This complementary task specialization typically pushes U.S.-born workers toward better-paying jobs, enhances the efficiency of production, and creates jobs. This task specialization, however, may involve adoption of different techniques or managerial procedures and the renovation or replacement of capital equipment. Hence, it takes some years to be fully realized.

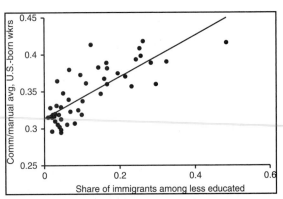

Figure 3   Communication/manual skills among less-educated U.S.-born workers

Note: The data on average communication/manual skills by state are from Peri and Sparber (2009), obtained from the manual and communication intensity of occupations, weighted according to the distributional occupation of U.S.-born workers.

Conclusions

The U.S. economy is dynamic, shedding and creating hundreds of thousands of jobs every month. Businesses are in a continuous state of flux. The most accurate way to gauge the net impact of immigration on such an economy is to analyze the effects dynamically over time. Data show that, on net, immigrants expand the U.S. economy's productive capacity, stimulate investment, and promote specialization that in the long run boosts productivity. Consistent with previous research, there is no evidence that these effects take place at the expense of jobs for workers born in the United States.

References

Borjas, George J. 2006. "Native Internal Migration and the Labor Market Impact of Immigration." *Journal of Human Resources* 41(2), pp. 221–258.

Card, David. 2001. "Immigrant Inflows, Native Outflows, and the Local Labor Market Impacts of Higher Immigration." *Journal of Labor Economics* 19(1), pp. 22–64.

Card, David. 2007. "How Immigration Affects U.S. Cities." University College London, Centre for Research and Analysis of Migration Discussion Paper 11/07.

Card, David. 2009. "Immigration and Inequality." *American Economic Review, Papers and Proceedings* 99(2), pp. 1–21.

Card, David, and Ethan Lewis. 2007. "The Diffusion of Mexican Immigrants during the 1990s: Explanations and Impacts." In *Mexican Immigration to the United States,* ed. George J. Borjas. Chicago: The University of Chicago Press.

Peri, Giovanni, and Chad Sparber. 2009. "Task Specialization, Immigration, and Wages." *American Economic Journal: Applied Economics* 1(3), pp. 135–169.

Peri, Giovanni. 2009. "The Effect of Immigration on Productivity: Evidence from U.S. States." NBER Working Paper 15507.

Critical Thinking

1. How can we put the immigrant challenge in perspective?
2. What is the link between the short-term and long-term effects on the economy and immigrant inflows?

Create Central

www.mhhe.com/createcentral

Internet References

www.frbsf.org/publications/economics/letter/2010/el2010-26.html

www.time.com/time/magazine/article/0,9171,1630543,00.html

http://immigrationnewstoday.com/the-effect-of-immigrants-on-u-s-employment-and-productivity

www.weeklystandard.com/articles/amnesty-next-time_722057.html

GIOVANNI PERI is an associate professor at the University of California, Davis, and a visiting scholar at the Federal Reserve Bank of San Francisco.

Peri, Giovanni. Reprinted with permission from the *FRBSF Economic Letter*, August 30, 2010. The opinions expressed in this article do not necessarily reflect the views of the management of the Federal Reserve Bank of San Francisco, or of the Board of Governors of the Federal Reserve System. www.frbsf.org/publications/economics/letter/2010/el2010–26.html

Article   Prepared by: Sudip Ghosh, *Penn State University—Berks*

Virtual Health Care Gaining Ground

CAROL GORGA WILLIAMS

Learning Outcomes

After reading this article, you will be able to:

- Explain how multimedia technology is changing the healthcare industry.

- See the advent of multimedia replacing face-to-face meetings with virtual meetings.

Technology is going to radically change your office visit to the doctor in the years ahead.

An "office" may not even be associated with your visit.

You may already have seen the changes: Your doctor allows you to make your next appointment online or when you arrive at your doctor's office, you sign in on an iPad instead of a clipboard.

In some states, physicians already conduct office visits via personal communication devices, using Skype, FaceTime, email or text.

Eventually, your doctor's visit will go something like this:

Your doctor reviews your test results on his laptop or handheld device in the examining room. As he listens to your concerns, he can access laboratory results from a facility five states away. Then, instead of reaching for that little blue pad to write a prescription, he quickly taps his computer and it is filed digitally to your pharmacy. As you drive home, your cellphone beeps: The pharmacy has alerted you that your prescription is ready. No matter how far technology advances, however, you are still going to wait on line there.

Larry Downs, the chief executive officer of the Medical Society of New Jersey, was just one of many who likened the end result of the electronic revolution in health care to the way the practice of medicine was portrayed on the original "Star Trek" series where Dr. McCoy often worked alone, aided largely by a single small device that could not only diagnose but also treat the patient.

The more radical applications of telemedicine are probably 10 years or more away here, experts say. Telemedicine has evolved more quickly in states and regions that are largely rural where finding a medical specialist is difficult and often involves a lengthy wait for an appointment.

"Some of my patients are already asking, 'Can I have a copy of my blood test today?' and I can print it right out for them," said Dr. John D. Gumina, founding member of the Jersey Shore Monmouth Family Medicine Group and chairman of Jersey Shore University Medical Center's Family Practice department. "I like it because patients are becoming more involved in their care. This is especially true of seniors who like to be kept updated."

The technology will mature very quickly, said those who are on the front lines now.

"We can take into account every patient at risk, and we will have the tools available to tell patients how they are doing," said Dr. Anthony D. Slonim, chief medical officer of Barnabas Health. "They are in the game now."

There are pilot programs that health systems can join. Some pilot programs use special computers that allow physicians in remote locations to take vital signs, have real-time conversations with patients and potentially improve outcomes by having specialists see patients promptly, even over long distances. That, in turn, means a faster, more accurate diagnosis for which treatment can begin more rapidly. Less waiting and fewer duplicate medical tests may mean more economical and less physically intrusive practice of medicine.

Nine states require a special license for the practice of telemedicine. Thirteen states have some form of telemedicine legislation under consideration.

"I think it is timely now," said Mishael Azam, senior manager for legislative services at the Medical Society of New Jersey. "I think people in health care are starting to talk about it. We have the technology now."

Electronic Data

According to 2012 data from an annual survey by the federal Centers for Disease Control and Prevention, 72 percent of office-based physicians used electronic medical record or electronic health record systems, up from 48 percent in 2009. Such record-keeping use ranged from 54 percent in New Jersey to 89 percent in Massachusetts.

Electronic record-keeping will become almost universally available within the next few years. Physicians face monetary penalties from the federal government if they don't comply. The same is true of electronic prescriptions. Physicians will have no choice. The little blue pads will be history.

With more accessible health care information, physicians will be able to detect health care patterns.

Carol Nering, a registered nurse from Toms River, N.J., who has been a longtime patient of Dr. Diane G. Verga, said the electronic medical record has its pluses and minuses.

"I personally am a little uncomfortable with it because I know anyone can hack into a computer," said Nering, 78. "I don't think you are really secure with" the way the information is stored and protected.

Still, Nering said, "in the computer, the information is easily read and that saves time, and unfortunately, in some instances, time is of the essence."

What About Malpractice?

While many physicians say it will probably reduce costs over the long term, one component of telemedicine practice still is the focus of debate and study. With telemedicine crossing state lines and with medical licenses still very much up to the states, how will questions of malpractice be handled?

"As the use of telemedicine grows, malpractice claims relating to telemedicine services may increase and, if so, these complications are likely to create a new body of law," the University of Maryland School of Law concluded in 2010. "As the specter of telemedicine-related claims grows, the professional liability industry is studying how to write and price medical malpractice policies for telemedicine practitioners."

The issue is complex. Telemedicine crosses state lines. Which state would have jurisdiction? Should a physician be held to the same standard of care as in face-to-face appointments? If a case goes bad, is the physician responsible or is it a failure of the technology as in the case of a lost Internet connection? Should telemedicine be its own category of malpractice law? What about informed consent from patients?

At this intersection of the age-old practice of medicine and the rapid development of technology, how malpractice and negligence questions will shake out is anyone's guess, the law school study summarized.

Technology's Help

But what does not seem to be in question is whether telemedicine can help make sick people better. The federal Department of Health and Human Services Office of Health Information Technology—which is overseeing the digital transformation of health care—says the medical applications of telemedicine helps patients, especially those who prefer to stay in their homes as they battle chronic conditions. And the government says the evidence demonstrates the quality of telemedicine.

Technology appears to help mitigate human error, which kills about 98,000 people every year, according to the American Association for Justice, a trial-lawyers' consumer group. The U.S. Department of Health and Human Services said 64 percent of physicians using electronic health record software properly were alerted to potential medication errors while 62 percent of physicians were informed of a critical laboratory test finding, thanks to the software.

Telemedicine, digital doctoring, telehealth, e-health, cybermedicine—whatever it'll be called—is appealing to physicians and their patients as insurers become more supportive. When Medicare pays, private insurers typically follow suit, and Medicare is authorizing reimbursement of telemedicine in limited ways, officials said.

"People are going to be seen by their doctor, either there or through a digital application," said Dr. Paul Katz, founding dean of Cooper Medical School of Rowan University in Camden, N.J. "Now we must figure out a way to manage it, a way that is not excessive and unnecessary."

Critical Thinking

1. How does virtual meeting allow for reducing costs?
2. Is telemedicine the way to go for remote and rural areas?
3. How can we engage the consumer in telemedicine?

Create Central

www.mhhe.com/createcentral

Internet References

www.news-medical.net/health/What-is-Telemedicine.aspx

www.healthcareitnews.com/news/st-louis-virtual-care-center-expand-telehealth-jobs

www.modernhealthcare.com/article/20130410/NEWS/304109960

http://usatoday30.usatoday.com/money/industries/health/story/2012-04-27/virtual-doctors-telemedicine/54791506/1

http://health.usnews.com/health-news/articles/2012/07/24/pros-and-cons-of-telemedicine-for-todays-workers

Article

Prepared by: Sudip Ghosh, *Penn State University—Berks*

Reaching Out to Dropouts

Those who find diplomas still matter are being shown innovative new paths.

STACY TEICHER KHADAROO

Learning Outcomes

After reading this article, you will be able to:

- Explain why a high school diploma is important.
- See how high school is using strategies to encourage students to stay in school.

Cydmarie Quinones dropped out of Boston's English High School in May 2011—senior year.

"It was the usual boyfriend story," she says. "You put so much attention into your relationship . . . that it kind of messes up the whole school thing."

Six classes shy of the credits she needed, she thought that she could skip getting a diploma and still find a college that would train her to be a medical assistant.

"I've been doing nothin' for a whole year," Ms. Quinones says. Actually, she's been running into walls—spending hundreds of dollars on in-person and online programs that made false promises to get her a high school credential.

Meanwhile, her friends graduated and went on to college, including her boyfriend. This fall, she says he told her, " 'I can't have a girlfriend that didn't do nothin' in life.' " So she decided, "OK . . . I have to do it for myself and for everybody else. . . . I have to get my diploma."

Nationally, about 600,000 students drop out of high school in a given year. And more than 5.8 million 16-to-24-year-olds are "disconnected"—not in school and not working. In 2011, governmental support (such as food stamps) and lost tax revenues associated with disconnected youths cost taxpayers more than $93.7 billion, according to Measure of America, an initiative of the Social Science Research Council, a nonprofit based in New York.

"Education has become so key to getting into the labor market [that] we call dropping out 'committing economic suicide' at this point," says Kathy Hamilton, youth transitions director for the Boston Private Industry Council, which partners with the school district to run the Boston Re-Engagement Center (REC), a hub for helping dropouts like Quinones complete their education.

Dropout prevention has been in the spotlight in recent years. But increasingly, school districts are also realizing that they can do more to bring young adults back into the fold.

It's called "dropout recovery," with districts deploying a host of strategies—from door-to-door searches for dropouts to alternative schools where people earn free college credits while taking their final high school courses. The efforts are taking place in dozens of cities ranging from Camden, N.J., to Alamo, Texas.

America has "long had a forgiving education system, where people can come back at any time to complete a diploma or finish a degree, but we haven't been structured to reach out and reengage youth who have dropped out," says Elizabeth Grant, chief of staff in the US Office of Elementary and Secondary Education. "As educators across the country saw more-accurate graduation and dropout numbers and recognized the size of the challenge, our school systems started to get more responsive."

The US Department of Education launched the High School Graduation Initiative in 2010 to support school districts doing dropout prevention and recovery work. Competitive grants were given out to 27 districts and two states, for a total of just under $50 million.

A Personalized Approach

At least 15 cities have organized stand-alone reengagement centers. They offer a one-stop, personalized case-management approach—bringing together schools, private businesses, workforce-development experts, and other partners to try to reconnect young adults with a promising future.

Since 2008, New York City's centers have reenrolled about 17,000 students, and the centers in Newark, N.J., have brought back 3,900, according to the National League of Cities.

Staff members at Boston's REC listen to each student's story, share struggles from their own school days, help them find the right school or alternative program to fit their needs, and stay in touch once they've reenrolled.

That's what won the trust of Quinones. In November she started coming every weekday to take online credit recovery courses at the REC, a bare-bones set of offices and computer labs with inspirational posters.

High School Graduation Rates

The end of the 2010–11 school year marked the first time states and the District of Columbia had to use a new common formula to report high school graduation rates. Now states can be compared based on how well they get students to an on-time high school diploma.

Starting with the 2011–12 data, the rates are to be used for the purposes of accountability under No Child Left Behind.

The rate reflects the percentage of students who earn a regular high school diploma in four years. Previously, some states counted students who earned GEDs or certificates of completion for special education. Schools also have to account for all students unless they can prove a student transferred to another school, moved out of the United States, or died.

While many of those who don't finish in four years are high school dropouts, there are also students who earn their diploma after five or six years—figures that some states choose to report in addition to the four-year rate.

The rates shown here, reported by the US Department of Education in November 2012, are "provisional." Final numbers will be released at some point this year, at which time an accurate national graduation rate figure should be available.

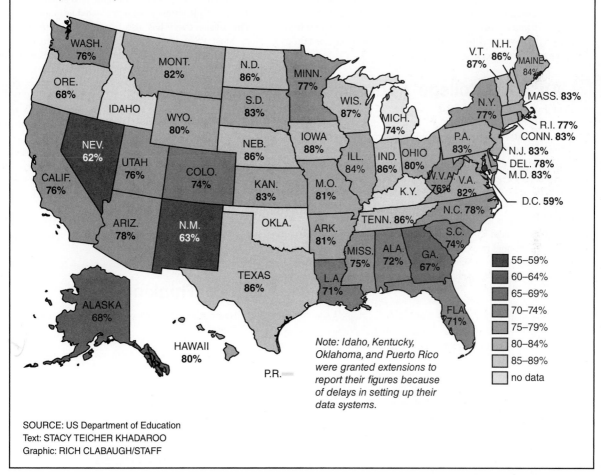

Note: Idaho, Kentucky, Oklahoma, and Puerto Rico were granted extensions to report their figures because of delays in setting up their data systems.

SOURCE: US Department of Education
Text: STACY TEICHER KHADAROO
Graphic: RICH CLABAUGH/STAFF

In just a month—keeping normal school hours, though that's not required—Quinones finished four courses and is on track to earn her diploma in February. Although she feels "stuck" in geometry, a teacher is on hand to guide her.

"In high school, teachers never really sat with me. . . . Having teachers take out their time . . . to go through one problem for four hours, that means a lot," she says.

The REC "has expertly directed students toward options that are best suited to their needs, rather than falling into the habit of putting them back in the school where they were previously unsuccessful," says Chad d'Entremont, executive director of the Rennie Center for Education Research & Policy in Cambridge, Mass.

Since 2010, the REC has reenrolled more than 1,300 students. About 7 out of 10 persist for at least a year. The tracking system for the total number of graduates is still being developed, but at least 160 earned their diploma within about a year, Ms. Hamilton says, and she predicts many more will do so over a longer time frame.

Dropouts are a diverse and difficult group to get across the finish line. About 1 in 5 says he or she lacks parental support, and another fifth are parents themselves, according to the 2012 High School Dropouts in America survey by Harris Interactive. Other reasons for dropping out include mental illness, the need to work, too many school absences, and uninteresting classes. Some dropouts have spent time in prison or on the streets.

Settings that offer flexible schedules and sustained personal attention are often required to help them master the skills they need.

"I'm always very honest with them: 'It's going to be tough, but it doesn't mean it's going to be impossible. And I'm going to help you envision yourself with a cap and gown a year from today, or two years from today,'" says Carolina Garcia, a dropout recovery specialist at Boston's REC.

An 'Early College' Approach

In Texas, an "early college" approach to dropout recovery is gaining national attention.

At least 10 districts are motivating dropouts to come back not just to finish high school, but also to take community-college courses free of charge—sometimes enough to earn an associate's degree or a training certificate.

The most notable is the Pharr-San Juan-Alamo district (PSJA), where 90 percent of the population is Hispanic and about a third is low income.

When Daniel King became superintendent there in 2007, he faced a dropout rate of about 18 percent. Nearly half the dropouts that year were seniors—237 of them. "I felt I needed to immediately do something . . . [because] the more time that went by, the harder it would be to find them and reengage them," he says.

In a matter of weeks, he had teamed up with South Texas College to launch the College, Career, & Technology Academy (CCTA) for 18-to-26-year-olds—in leased space in a former Wal-Mart.

He put up banners around town with the message: "You didn't finish high school. Start college today." That, combined with a door-to-door search for students who had dropped out, resulted in 223 of those seniors coming back to school.

By May 2008, about 130 had earned their diplomas. To date, more than 1,000 students have graduated from CCTA, more than half of them with college credits.

Along with core academic courses, former dropouts start with a college-success course that solidifies their study skills. Then they move on to career and technical-education courses such as welding or medical terminology.

The state allows both the school district and the community college to receive per-pupil funding, so the education at CCTA is free to students. Texas is also unique in funding high school students up to age 26. (Most states stop at around 21.)

"Before I came to this school, I had zero drive in me," says CCTA student Edgar Rodriguez. He was out of school for a semester and a summer while being "reckless" and "irresponsible," he says.

At CCTA, teachers tutored him for exams that had previously stumped him. The college-success class, taught by his former English teacher, inspired him to want to pursue teaching.

During a recent visit to an elementary school, Mr. Rodriguez shared a story and Web page he had created. "I had never been on that other side of the table where I was the one giving the presentation. I loved the atmosphere," he says. "I knew then, that's what I want to do."

As a fallback, he's taken medical-billing classes. His older brother was the first in the family to graduate from high school, he says. "Now I hope to lay down the next standard of going to college," says Rodriguez, who graduated last month.

Dropout recovery has also inspired more-effective prevention. Most PSJA students now have access to college-level courses while still in high school, which keeps them motivated. And students falling behind in the regular schools can move into "transition communities" where they get more individualized attention until they catch up.

The district's dropout rate is dramatically down—from 18 percent in 2006 to just 3.1 percent in 2011. (The state average was 6.8 percent in 2011.)

Superintendent King was able to expand the early-college approach because "he made the case [that] if these [former dropouts] can go to college, why can't we do this for all students?" says Lili Allen, who is helping a network of districts replicate PSJA's approach.

"It was a smart and counterintuitive strategy," adds Ms. Allen, director of Back on Track Designs at Jobs for the Future, a nonprofit based in Boston.

Critical Thinking

1. How can we help to reduce the number of high school dropouts?
2. What kind of costs do high school dropouts incur on society?
3. How can we engage the at-risk high school students so that they can even receive college credits?

Create Central

www.mhhe.com/createcentral

Internet References

www.nytimes.com/2012/01/26/opinion/the-true-cost-of-high-school-dropouts.html

www.nga.org/cms/home/nga-center-for-best-practices/center-issues/page-edu-issues/col2-content/main-content-list/dropout-prevention--recovery.html

www.nea.org/assets/docs/HE/dropoutguide1108.pdf

www.usnews.com/education/blogs/high-school-notes/2011/10/03/new-report-details-high-school-dropout-prevention-efforts

Article   Prepared by: Sudip Ghosh, *Penn State University—Berks*

The GED Test Gets a Makeover

Questions on the test will pose real-world problems.

Stacy Teicher Khadaroo

Learning Outcomes

After reading this article, you will be able to:

- Explain the contribution of GED-holders.

- Understand why GED-holders tend not to do better than high school dropouts with no GED.

An estimated 40 million US adults have not finished high school.

Every year, about 800,000 people take GED tests, and more than 400,000 succeed in earning the GED, a high school equivalency credential that's recognized in all 50 states.

But "the value of the GED is in question," says Jonathan Zaff, director of the Center for Promise, a research center based at Tufts University in Medford, Mass., and sponsored by America's Promise Alliance, a youth-advocacy coalition.

Some research finds that, economically, GED-holders tend to fare about as well as high school dropouts with no GED, Mr. Zaff says. That may be one reason the GED is undergoing a transformation—the biggest in its 70-year history. And it's stirring up controversy along the way.

The new test is designed "to embrace the college- and career-readiness standards" that states have been adopting, says Randy Trask, president of GED Testing Service in Washington.

The test will roll out in January 2014, so people preparing for the current GED have just under a year to finish up.

Test-takers will be required to show how they can use what they've learned to solve real-world problems, Mr. Trask says. Also, the test will be computerized, he says, a delivery system that some states have already begun to adopt.

The plans have raised concerns about educational access—especially since the new tests, as well as a new cost structure, coincide with a private company becoming involved in the GED tests for the first time.

The GED has traditionally been run by the American Council on Education, a nonprofit higher-education association in Washington. In March 2011 it partnered with Pearson, a for-profit provider of educational materials and services, to form the new GED Testing Service.

That "raised some red flags for us," says Wade Henderson, president and chief executive officer of The Leadership Conference on Civil and Human Rights, a coalition based in Washington.

The GED "is a gatekeeper to opportunity for our most poor and most vulnerable citizens," he says. "It needs to be strengthened and aligned to current core standards . . . but it won't succeed if the costs are too high."

Costs for taking the test ranges from nothing to as much as $200 or more, depending on where test-takers live. The cost of the new computerized test will be $120; but as before, how much of that is passed on to test-takers will vary. Moreover, it's unclear whether the price will go up after 2014.

Out of 26 states that set prices, 25 charge less than $120, according to the National Council of State Directors of Adult Education.

Mr. Henderson also wonders if all testing centers can make the transition from pencil and paper to computers in time and prepare non-computer-savvy students.

The new system might save states money. Under the old cost model, they leased the test and had to pay for oversight and grading themselves, Trask says.

The new price reflects a centralization of costs. Discussions should be under way at the federal, state, and local levels, he says, about how to ensure that those most in need can take GED tests.

The next step, Trask says, is connecting the GED with more pathways into college or vocational training. For instance, he's hoping to develop bridge courses between the GED and certifications in the information technology industry.

Critical Thinking

1. How do high school drop outs who take the GED often excel?
2. Why have concerns been raised about cost structures of GED providers?
3. Should private or public entities be responsible for administering GED exams?

Create Central

www.mhhe.com/createcentral

Internet References

www.econ.wisc.edu/Durlauf/HHR.pdf

http://pewhispanic.org/files/reports/122.pdf

http://performanceassessment.org/articles/pa_moreyouths.html

www.hks.harvard.edu/inequality/Summer/Summer99/privatepapers/Murnane.PDF

Article

Prepared by: Sudip Ghosh, *Penn State University—Berks*

13 States Raising Pay for Minimum-Wage Workers

State minimum wages will exceed the federal minimum of $7.25 an hour in 21 states on January 1

Paul Davidson

Learning Outcomes

After reading this article, you will be able to:

• Define the current minimum wage.

• Discuss the new raise in the minimum wage.

• Understand the difference between state and federal minimum wage.

The retail-worker strikes that swept the nation in 2013 did not move Congress to raise the minimum wage, but a growing number of states are taking action.

The minimum wage will rise in 13 states this week, and as many as 11 states and Washington, D.C., are expected to consider increases in 2014, according to the National Employment Law Project. Approval is likely in more than half of the 11, says NELP policy analyst Jack Temple.

The trend reflects growing concerns about the disproportionate spread of low-wage jobs in the U.S. economy, creating millions of financially strained workers and putting too little money in consumers' pockets to spur faster economic growth.

On January 1, state minimum wages will be higher than the federal requirement of $7.25 an hour in 21 states, up from 18 two years ago. Temple expects another nine states to drift above the federal minimum by the end of 2014, marking the first time minimum pay in most states will be above the federal level.

"2014 is poised to be a turning point," Temple says. "States are seeing the unemployment rate is going down but job growth is disproportionately concentrated in low-wage industries. (They're) frustrated that Congress is dragging its feet."

Connecticut, New York, New Jersey, and Rhode Island legislatures voted to raise the minimum hourly wage by as much as $1, to $8 to $8.70, by Wednesday. In California, a $1 increase to $9 is scheduled on July 1. Smaller automatic increases tied to inflation will take effect in nine other states: Arizona, Colorado, Florida, Missouri, Montana, Ohio, Oregon, Vermont, and Washington.

Meanwhile, states such as Massachusetts, New Hampshire, Maryland, Minnesota, and South Dakota plan to weigh minimum-wage hikes next year through legislation or ballot initiatives.

In Minnesota, the state House and Senate have each passed bills to raise the minimum wage and plan to iron out their differences early next year after failing to approve similar measures the past two decades.

"You're coming out of a deep recession, and people are landing jobs, but they're low-paid," says state Rep. Ryan Winkler, sponsor of the House bill.

The legislative movement has been partly fueled by walkouts this year in at least 100 cities by fast-food workers who are calling for $15-an-hour pay and the right to form unions. Wal-Mart workers have staged similar protests.

While the demonstrations were not explicitly intended to prompt minimum pay increases, they've made the issue "more urgent," Temple says.

The Bureau of Labor Statistics estimates that 3.6 million hourly paid workers received wages at or below the federal minimum in 2012—almost 5 percent of all employees on hourly pay schedules.

President Obama recently said he supports legislation in Congress that would lift the federal minimum wage to $10.10 an hour in three steps over two years and then index it to inflation. But the measure faces an uphill climb in Congress.

Proponents of minimum-wage hikes note that low-wage jobs have dominated payroll growth in the 4-year-old recovery, and increases over the past four decades have not kept pace with inflation.

Opponents say the increases raise employer expenses and will lead to layoffs. "If your costs are going up and you can't raise prices, you have to find a way to produce the same product at a lower cost," says Michael Saltsman, a research fellow at the Employment Policies Institute.

Where Minimum Wage is Going Up

On January 1, the minimum wage in 13 states will increase to these amounts.

State	New minimum wage ($)
Arizona	7.90
Colorado	8.00
Connecticut	8.70
Florida	7.93
Missouri	7.50
Montana	7.90
New Jersey	8.25
New York	8.00
Ohio	7.95
Oregon	9.10
Rhode Island	8.00
Vermont	8.73
Washington	9.32

Critical Thinking

1. Why is it important to raise state minimum wage?
2. What are the pros and cons of raising state minimum wage?

Create Central

www.mhhe.com/createcentral

Internet References

TIME
http://business.time.com/2013/12/30/minimum-wage-to-rise-in-13-states-in-2014/

PBS Newshour
http://www.pbs.org/newshour/rundown/14-million-workers-get-minimum-wage-raise/

Politicus USA
http://www.politicususa.com/2013/12/28/happy-year-minimum-wage-workers-13-states-automatic-pay-raise.html

Unit 4

UNIT

Prepared by: Sudip Ghosh, *Penn State University—Berks*

Macroeconomics

Macroeconomics encompasses the functioning of the entire economy. Macroeconomists develop models to explain the links among national income, output, consumption, unemployment, inflation, savings, investment, economic growth, etc. It shows how government policies are used to promote economic growth, mitigate unemployment, and stabilize general level of prices in the economy. Before 1930s, most economists (known as "classicists") believed that free market capitalism was the road to prosperity and economy was capable of achieving those goals without government intervention. One of the basic tenets of classical economics was full employment equilibrium. Classical economist had a difficult time to defend its claim

during the Great Depression where unemployment soared to 25 percent, followed by a period of prolonged and widespread joblessness, falling incomes, bankruptcies, and political turmoil. In 1936, British economist John Maynard Keynes attacked the classical view in his *General Theory of Employment, Interest, and Money* and how macroeconomic goals achieved through fiscal responsibility and active government participation. In later year's monetarism (Milton Friedman), new classical economics (Robert Lucas) also gained prominence. Supply-side economics (Arthur Laffer) became popular during the Reagan administration, where reduction in marginal tax rates stimulate economic wellbeing.

Article   Prepared by: Sudip Ghosh, *Penn State University—Berks*

Unemployment Rate

Kimberly Amadeo

Learning Outcomes

After reading this article, you will be able to:

- Understand BLS.
- Define real unemployment rate.
- Define structural unemployment rate.

What the Unemployment Rate Measures?

The unemployment rate is the number in the civilian labor force divided by the number of unemployed. However, everyone without a job isn't necessarily unemployed, at least according to the Bureau of Labor Statistics (BLS). To be counted in the unemployment rate, you not only have to be without a job, you have to have actively looked for work in the past four weeks. If you were temporarily laid off and are waiting to be called back to that job, you're still counted. If you've given up looking for work, you're not counted in the unemployment rate. Many people argue that the real unemployment rate is much higher, since it should count those discouraged workers.

The unemployment rate is reported by the BLS on the first Friday of each month. It is useful to compare this month's unemployment rate compared to that of the same month last year, or year-over-year. This rules out the effects of seasonality. If you only compare this month's unemployment rate to last month's, it could be higher because of something that always happens that month, such as the school year ending. It may not indicate an ongoing trend.

How the Unemployment Rate Affects the U.S. Economy?

Obviously, the unemployment rate is important as a gauge of joblessness. For this reason, it's also a gauge of the economy's growth rate.

However, the unemployment rate is a lagging indicator. This means it measures the *effect* of economic events, such as a recession. The unemployment rate doesn't rise until after a recession has already started. It also means the unemployment rate will continue to rise even after the economy has started to recover.

Why is that? Employers are reluctant to lay people off when the economy turns bad. For large companies, it can take months to put together a layoff plan. Companies are even more reluctant to hire new workers until they are sure the economy are well into the expansion phase of the business cycle. During the 2008 financial crisis, the recession actually started in the first quarter of 2008, when GDP fell 1.8 percent. The unemployment rate didn't reach 5.5 percent until May 2008. It reached its peak of 10.2 percent in October 2009, after the recession had ended. In the 2001 recession, unemployment went from 5.6 percent in 2002 to 6 percent in 2003, even though the recession ended in 2002.

For that reason, the unemployment rate is a powerful confirmation of what the other indicators are already showing. For example, if the other indicators show an expanding economy, *and* the unemployment rate is declining, then you know for sure businesses are confident enough to start hiring again. See how this worked in U.S Unemployment Rate by Year.

The unemployment rate is an important indicator the Federal Reserve uses to determine the health of the economy when setting monetary policy. Investors also use current unemployment statistics to look at which sectors are losing jobs faster. They can then determine which sector-specific mutual funds to sell.

How the Unemployment Rate Affects You?

The year-over-year unemployment rate will tell you if unemployment is worsening. If more people are looking for work, less people will be buying, and the retail sector will decline. Also, if you are unemployed yourself, it will tell you how much competition you have, and how much leverage you might have in negotiating for a new position. When the unemployment rate reaches 6–7 percent, as it did in 2008, the government gets concerned, and tries to create jobs through stimulating the economy. It may also extend unemployment benefits to prevent the recession from deepening. Studies show that extended unemployment benefits are the best way to boost the economy. Monetary policy can also be used to lower unemployment. For more, see Unemployment Solutions.

Recent Unemployment Trends

Unemployment peaked at 10.2 percent in October 2009. It rose steadily from its low of 4.4 percent in March 2007. It did not really become a concern until a year later when it broke above 5 percent in March 2008. By then, the economy had contracted. The unemployment rate rose rapidly, breaking 6.2 percent in August 2008, 7.2 percent by November 2008, 8.1 percent by February 2009, 9.4 percent three months later, finally reaching 10.2 percent in October.

The recession may have caused a new natural rate of unemployment because of all the long-term unemployed. This creates a high structural unemployment rate, since their job skills no longer match the new jobs being created.

Unemployment hadn't been so high since the 1981 recession, when it above 10 percent for 10 months. During the 2001 recession, the unemployment rate peaked at 6.3 percent in June 2003. (Source: BLS, Historical Tables)

Critical Thinking

1. Who is responsible for calculating U.S. unemployment rate every month?
2. How does the unemployment rate affect the U.S. economy?
3. Why do individuals sometimes question the way unemployment is calculated?

Create Central

www.mhhe.com/createcentral

Internet References

Bloomberg Business Week
http://www.businessweek.com/articles/2014-01-20/how-killing-unemployment-benefits-could-kill-economic-growth

Congressional Research Service
http://fas.org/sgp/crs/misc/R42063.pdf

Economics Help
http://www.economicshelp.org/blog/10142/unemployment/low-economic-growth-unemployment/

Article

Prepared by: Sudip Ghosh, *Penn State University—Berks*

What Threat Do the Monetary Policies of Developed Nations Pose to Emerging Economies?

RONAN KEENAN

Learning Outcomes

After reading this article, you will be able to:

- Understand currency depreciation.
- Identify G7/G20 countries.
- Understand fiscal expansion.

There will be no currency wars. Or so the G7 tried to say in February. A week later the G20 released a similar statement claiming its nations will not target their exchange rates in search of a competitive edge. Yet the message was deemed too vague by financial markets and did little to ease concerns from emerging economies that their growth will be hampered by monetary policies of major developed nations.

Emerging markets have garnered much attention in the aftermath of the 2008 financial crisis as their improving infrastructure, competitive edge, and strong growth potential attracted investment from the developed world. A relatively weaker currency is a key tool for emerging economies as it makes their exports more appealing to developed nations that have stronger purchasing power.

So it was with little surprise that officials in numerous emerging economies reacted with cynicism late last year when new Japanese premier Shinzo Abe called for a weaker yen to boost his nation's exports and revealed plans to spur growth by increasing Japan's money supply through the purchasing of government bonds. The yen has consequently depreciated sharply across the board. The U.S. Federal Reserve and Bank of England also utilize similar stimulus measures, albeit without directly stating their desire for a weaker currency.

Comparatively high inflationary pressures in many emerging economies prevent them from adopting comparable policies. As a result, there has been anxiety that emerging economies will react to any significant strengthening of their own currencies by launching large-scale intervention in markets to artificially manipulate exchange rates while also adopting "beggar-thy-neighbor" policies that could disrupt global growth.

The "currency war" terminology was first used by Brazil's finance minister in 2010 regarding the Federal Reserve's quantitative easing—the buying of bonds with newly created money. The phrase was reignited in January by the Russian central bank when it accused Japan of potentially instigating "very serious, confrontational actions." In February, the president of China's sovereign-wealth fund advised Japan against using its neighbors as a "garbage bin" by deliberately devaluing the yen. Later, several of South Korea's biggest companies warned that a stronger domestic currency will lead to significant deterioration in profits.

Fears have been compounded by some economists cautioning that reactionary devaluations could lead to a similar scenario that occurred following the removal of the gold standard in the 1930s. At that time, nations engaged in devaluations against each other and ultimately introduced trade barriers and protectionist policies that dislocated trade and segregated the global economy. Several countries such as Brazil and South Korea have already introduced controls to reduce speculative capital flows that may strengthen their currencies.

A depreciation in currency value will be a short-term consequence of Japan's policies and will likely have a negative impact on its smaller neighbors who trade in similar export markets. The possibility of lost jobs in manufacturing sectors is understandably difficult for political leaders in developing nations to accept. Yet despite this short-term prospect, the likelihood of a currency war scenario is exaggerated. The U.S., Japan, and UK are not intervening in currency markets. Their monetary stimulus efforts are not direct attempts to weaken their currencies; the intention is to lower domestic lending rates and boost spending at home.

Focusing on the policies of developed nations and overstating their threat gives authorities in emerging economies an opportunity to turn attention away from difficulties at home. The outlook for the major emerging economies is not as upbeat as in previous years. With further fiscal expansion unfeasible, China is incapable of sustaining rapid growth. A drop in Chinese demand will hurt the Brazilian economy, and a relaxation in monetary policy has left Brazil vulnerable to inflation risks. And while the Indian stock market is near record highs, the country is facing rising inflation, falling growth, and potential political uncertainty following elections next year. Russia has the potential to perform well, although it too has been dealing with increased inflation and a stubbornly high dependency on oil prices, leaving it with a precarious economic outlook. Looking past the alarming rhetoric, emerging economies actually have much to gain from stronger currencies. In the longer-term, buoyant major economies result in increased demand for their trading partners' output. Stronger emerging market currencies will give developing economies an opportunity to ease inflationary pressures while spurring domestic consumption by making imports cheaper, potentially driving companies to develop more innovative products which will spawn higher-paying jobs. Moreover, the extent of a weaker yen is unclear. The Bank of Japan will have a considerable amount of expansion to do if it is to bring the yen to a level that will have a truly lasting impact on its exports market. It would be remarkable if this year the yen weakened to its pre-2007 levels.

The G7/G8 has not done enough to help the situation. While the G7 statement in February said its nations would not target exchange rates, the message was too ambiguous as it made no reference to Japan. The group needs to clearly state that large-scale currency manipulation by its members will not be tolerated. Such measures can help dismiss currency war rhetoric, allowing leaders of emerging economies to focus on addressing their own policies.

Critical Thinking

1. How do policies of developed nations impact emerging markets?

2. What are risks of currency depreciation initiated by developed nations on emerging economies?

Create Central

www.mhhe.com/createcentral

Internet References

Council on Foreign Relations
http://www.cfr.org/monetary-policy/federal-reserve-policy-emerging-markets/p32184

The Economist
http://www.economist.com/blogs/freeexchange/2014/01/more-emerging-market-jitters

Federal Reserve Bank of New York
http://www.ny.frb.org/newsevents/speeches/2014/dud140327.html

Keenan, Ronan. From *G8 Summit 2013 Edition of The Official ICC G20 Advisory Group Publication*, October 2013. Copyright © 2013 International Chamber of Commerce. Reprinted with permission.

Article   Prepared by: Sudip Ghosh, *Penn State University—Berks*

Can Better Regulation Boost Growth?

MARK WEINBERGER

Learning Outcomes

After reading this article, you will be able to:

- Understand economic growth and its relationship to regulation.

- Define CAFE.

It has been called the "war of words." The disagreements over the Volcker rule between bankers and regulators have been well documented. It is one of the most recent and visible clashes between business and regulators. It is by no means the first or the last time the two groups will struggle to find common ground.

While it can sometimes seem that business and regulators are at odds, they can agree on one thing: the need for smooth functioning markets that allow business to invest in people and innovation thereby creating economic growth. Smarter regulation can help to achieve this.

Unfortunately, today's regulatory environment is characterized by a patchwork of complex, overlapping and often inconsistent rules. The US alone finalizes between 2,500 and 4,500 rules each year, according to the Congressional Research Service. The complexity is magnified for any business that operates across borders.

Governments need to work with the private sector to find the right balance between managing risk and allowing innovation to drive growth and employment.

Reducing regulatory burdens can have a real impact. The recent Bali agreement, which cuts red tape in relation to customs procedures and was brokered by the World Trade Organization, will, by some estimates, raise global output by more than US$ 400 billion a year.

However, the answer is not only to reduce the burden but also to ensure that regulations are well designed. During my career I've worked in both the private and public sectors. The experience of sitting on both sides of the table has given me an appreciation of the benefits of good regulation as well as a keen understanding of what an ideal regulatory framework should look like.

Well-designed regulation plays an important role in helping the markets function. Take for example US Corporate Average Fuel Economy (CAFE) standards. It helps to provide regulatory certainty to the US car industry and allows companies to invest in technologies that save an estimated three million gallons of oil a day.

The government negotiated with 13 carmakers that initially opposed the standards to win their support. This is a critical point: the regulatory process should invite, encourage, and consider the input of all interested parties. And the dialogue should continue once regulations are in place. There should be a process of ensuring that the effectiveness is continually evaluated.

Open communication between the business community and policy-makers is key. Businesses need to be open and responsive with policy-makers, and not just react. They need to not only answer the questions that have been asked but also to raise—and answer—new questions.

When thinking about regulations we should remember the challenges connected to their implementation and continued effectiveness. The implementation of Basel III has shown us that overlooked details can lead to unintended consequences. There is often the risk that regulations impose significant costs or alter behavior in unintended ways. This is particularly true if regulators lack strong technical knowledge. In the absence of knowledge, regulations may focus on the wrong areas or fail to evolve to take account of industry or market changes. This underscores the importance of reasonable flexibility.

Flexibility is necessary in both implementation and enforcement. Enforcement must be effective and focused on the right priorities. After all, regulation is only as good as the enforcement behind it.

In today's globally connected world enforcement is even trickier given the complexities that arise when businesses operate across borders. To be effective, governments must work together in all stages of the regulatory process from development to enforcement. The financial sector in particular needs both a globally consistent framework and a desire among countries to work together to create one. Institutions such as the Financial Stability Board, the Basel Committee, and the International Organization of Security Commissions have an important role to play.

I'm looking forward to taking part in a panel discussion, "Getting Back to Natural Growth," on Wednesday morning of this year's Annual Meeting where we'll be talking about regulation among other topics. It's a good follow-up to a really interesting discussion we had regarding regulatory frameworks at last September's World Economic Forum Annual Meeting of the New Champions.

Critical Thinking

1. How do good regulations boost economic growth?
2. What are some examples of regulations that the author alluded to in this article?
3. Why is flexibility an important part of regulation?

Create Central

www.mhhe.com/createcentral

Internet References

AE Ideas
http://www.aei-ideas.org/2013/06/federal-regulations-have-lowered-gdp-growth-by-2-per-year/

The World Bank eLibrary
http://elibrary.worldbank.org/doi/book/10.1596/1813-9450-3623

The Wall Street Journal
http://online.wsj.com/news/articles/SB10001424052702304049904579518793072183178

Article   Prepared by: Sudip Ghosh, *Penn State University—Berks*

Is the Border Secure?

The question may be key to immigration reform.

LOURDES MEDRANO

Learning Outcomes

After reading this article, you will be able to:

- Understand the challenges facing U.S. Border Security.

- Learn the economic impacts of the porous southern border.

Travelers on Interstate 19 don't need any "Welcome to Mexico" signs to know that the border is near. Twenty-five miles north of the line, a giant white canopy stretches over the north-bound lanes, with green-shirted border patrol agents and drug-sniffing dogs buzzing around the checkpoint. Farther south in Nogales, Ariz., green-and-white border patrol vehicles are as conspicuous as yellow cabs in New York, and stadium lights trained on the border fence dwarf the rustic Sonoran homes below.

Ten years ago, the permanent checkpoint, the stadium lights, and the ubiquity of those green-and-white cars would have seemed jarring. But since 9/11, America's southern border has changed. President George W. Bush's most famous surge might have been in Iraq, but along the US-Mexican border, he also presided over a doubling of manpower and a shift in the border patrol's mission to make it a tool in the war on terror.

Now, as Washington considers immigration reform, the border patrol and its mission are again in the spotlight. Many Republicans say reform, without increased border security, is a nonstarter. But Mr. Bush's surge offers lessons about what can realistically be accomplished—and what tops an unfinished to-do list.

Statistical and anecdotal evidence show there has been progress in reining in illegal immigration, most agree. But there have been unintended consequences, such as the rise in human trafficking to avert the border buildup. Moreover, many stakeholders remain divided about whether the border needs even more attention, or whether the United States should shift its focus on immigration-enforcement efforts inward.

"While we have made enormous progress in improving border security, the job is not finished," says Jessica Vaughan, director of policy studies at the Center for Immigration Studies, which advocates tighter border enforcement.

That sentiment is echoed by Republicans whose support could be crucial to immigration reform. During the first Senate hearing on the topic this year, GOP senators challenged the assertion by Department of Homeland Security Secretary Janet Napolitano that "our borders have, in fact, never been stronger."

Sen. John Cornyn (R) of Texas responded: "I do not believe the border is secure, and I still believe we have a long, long way to go."

Going forward, a central question in the immigration-reform debate will be what more can—and should—be done. In many ways, answering that question depends on understanding what has been done so far.

While the massive rise in illegal immigration throughout the 1980s and '90s brought some increases in manpower and technology to the Southwest border, 9/11 started a sea of change.

In 2003, the size of the border patrol stood at 10,717 agents. In 2012, the number totaled 21,394, with 18,516 stationed along a Southwest border reinforced with state-of-the-art technology that includes ground sensors, hand-held thermal-imaging equipment, surveillance cameras, and predator drones. During that time, the border patrol budget increased from $1.4 billion to $3.5 billion, according to agency data.

Those increases have been supplemented by other initiatives. In 2006, Bush signed the Secure Fence Act, which authorized 700 miles of fencing—as well as infrastructure such as vehicle barriers, roads, and checkpoints—along the 2,000-mile border with Mexico. The same year, the Bush administration endorsed plans for a "virtual fence" of surveillance equipment to run almost the entire length of the border.

The Secure Fence Act aimed to achieve "operational control" over the entire border, defining the phrase as "the prevention of all unlawful entries into the United States, including entries by terrorists, other unlawful aliens, instruments of terrorism, narcotics, and other contraband."

That, experts say, was an unrealistic expectation. There will never be a secure border by that definition, says Donald Kerwin, executive director at the Center for Migration Studies, which defends migrants' rights.

Even the Berlin Wall failed by that measure, he notes. "At that point they were shooting at unauthorized crossers," he says. "Even on a heavily fortified, militarized 37-mile wall, people were crossing. To think that nobody will cross illegally over a 2,000-mile border is fanciful."

In 2010, that realization—together with rising costs and technological challenges—led the Obama administration to kill the virtual fence.

Signs of Success

That doesn't mean the border surge was a failure, though.

Border patrol officials say a historic decline in total apprehensions nationwide—from a peak of 1.6 million in 2000 to 356,873 in 2012—is a sign of success. As further proof that the border is under control, the agency touts its record of intercepting a massive amount of smuggled drugs, and offers FBI statistics showing that crime is lower in border areas than in some parts of the US interior.

"The high-speed chases, the rollovers, the chaos that comes with a border out of control, that is no longer the norm," said Manuel Padilla, acting chief of the border patrol's Tucson sector, at a recent meeting. "That is no longer there."

The soft US economy has been a significant contributor to the drop in illegal entries—fewer jobs attract fewer immigrants. But other experts agree that the security surge has played a role in bringing apprehensions down to levels last seen in the early 1970s.

"The investments were really significant, and they had an effect," says Thad Bingel, former chief of staff for Customs and Border Protection in the Bush administration and a founding partner of Command Consulting Group, a security consultancy in Washington, D.C.

"It's much more difficult to cross the border in Arizona or California or Texas today than it was in 2005, and your chances of getting caught are much higher," he adds.

But that progress has come at a cost, some say. Congress's response to the 9/11 attacks not only changed the size of the border patrol but also its purpose. In 2003, when the border patrol became part of the newly created Department of Homeland Security (DHS), its mission was expanded to prioritize capturing terrorists and weapons of terror at the border.

Bringing the agency under DHS brought cohesiveness to the border effort, Mr. Bingel says. But "it did change the mind-set, and it did change the focus and the tools that were applied."

Joe Dassaro, a former border patrol agent, says the move made the agency's mission diffuse. "The agency was receiving mixed signals," he recalls. Agents were being told, "your only mission is to apprehend terrorists."

Too Much, Too Fast?

The sheer speed of the buildup also had negative consequences, Mr. Dassaro says. Agents were hired so quickly that training standards weakened. He became involved in his local union, and the more he studied the history of immigration policy, the more disillusioned he became about how it was being carried out. He left the agency in 2005.

In recent years, the border patrol has been under fire for excessive use of force, shootings involving agents, and corruption among its ranks. While those problems are "relatively few," says Louis DeSipio, a political scientist at the University of California at Irvine, they could be an outgrowth of claims of discrimination in border communities. "People who look like they're from Latin America are much more likely to face the wrath of the border patrol," he says.

There have been signs of progress. In El Paso, Texas, the Border Network for Human Rights reached out to the border patrol after people felt they were targets "because of the way they looked and the way they dressed." Complaints dropped significantly.

"What we did here is considered a success because the community and the border patrol worked together," says Fernando Garcia, the group's executive director.

Rise of People-Smuggling

The buildup also has changed how migrants cross the border. As the agency has made the trek north more difficult, more people have started crossing through remote regions of the desert and mountainous terrain. In Arizona alone, more than 2,400 people have died since 2000, according to Tucson human rights groups.

"The discussion of the deaths is not even included in border security, and it should be," says Raquel Rubio-Goldsmith, an immigrants rights activist.

The tightening of the border has also empowered organized crime to branch into the increasingly lucrative business of people-smuggling.

"They take $1,000, $2,000, $3,000 a pop for each migrant that they smuggle into the country, often in hideously dangerous conditions," said David Shirk, director of the Trans-Border Institute at the University of San Diego, in a teleconference.

Yesenia Mercado, who was deported through Nogales last month, says smugglers charged her $3,800 to guide her across the border—an amount relatives promised to pay once she made it to Los Angeles. She intends to cross again to join her US-born children, who stayed in California when she visited family in Mexico. "It's not as easy to get across as it once was," she says.

Still, a 2011 report by the Government Accountability Office (GAO) concluded that only 873 of the nearly 2,000 miles of the Southwest border were under "operational control." Some 129 of those miles were under "full control" with the remainder "managed."

This year, another GAO report concluded that the agency lacks specific milestones and timelines to establish metrics that accurately assess border security. Agency leaders say they are working to develop them, but the question remains an open one that is crucial to immigration reform: How does one measure success?

At first, the surge targeted areas with the greatest illicit traffic. In 2005, it tried to set out a quantifiable benchmark for success, defining "operational control" as "the ability to detect,

Border Patrol: Then and Now

Since 2001, the scope of the border patrol's operation along the US-Mexican border has ballooned, bringing with it new personnel, technology, and security. The agency says the plummeting number of border apprehensions is proof that it is succeeding at deterring illegal crossings.

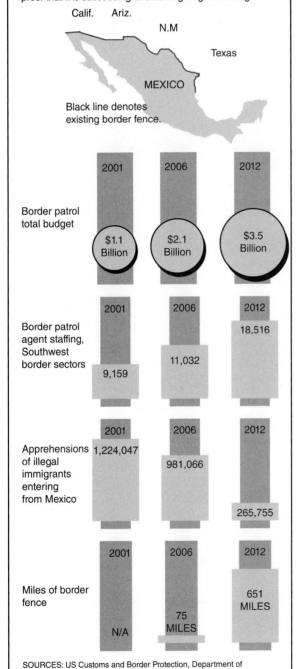

Calif.   Ariz.

N.M

Texas

MEXICO

Black line denotes existing border fence.

Border patrol total budget

2001	2006	2012
$1.1 Billion	$2.1 Billion	$3.5 Billion

Border patrol agent staffing, Southwest border sectors

2001	2006	2012
9,159	11,032	18,516

Apprehensions of illegal immigrants entering from Mexico

2001	2006	2012
1,224,047	981,066	265,755

Miles of border fence

2001	2006	2012
N/A	75 MILES	651 MILES

SOURCES: US Customs and Border Protection, Department of Homeland Security
Research: RYAN LENORA BROWN
Graphic: RICH CLABAUGH/STAFF

respond, and interdict border penetrations in areas deemed in high priorities for threat potential or other national security objectives."

But last year, the agency announced a new strategy, saying it would focus on repeat crossers and their intentions. For former agent Dassaro, the changes are evidence that the border patrol's objectives have become so abstract that "nobody knows what success is."

Prescriptions for success vary widely.

The district of Rep. Ron Barber (D) of Arizona is, in many ways, at the center of the immigration debate. It is part of the Tucson sector, which for years has been the most popular gateway for illegal immigration. In the rolling hills and high desert grasslands, where agents say rough terrain makes access difficult, veterinarian Gary Thrasher carries a gun when he travels to ranches near the border.

"The ranchers on the border have to put up with a huge amount of [illegal] traffic," says Mr. Thrasher, who wants more agents.

Congressman Barber sounds a similar note. In 2010, Congress approved $600 million for border security and sent 500 National Guard troops to Arizona, but too many border crossers and drugs are still getting through, he says. In his view, the border patrol needs to get better at using its resources effectively.

"We've got a long, long fence or wall across most of the border in my district, but it's not patrolled," Barber says. "Most of the time there's nobody on it in terms of personnel. So is it effective? Not really because people go over it and cut through it."

Looking Inward

But others say now is the time to turn attention inward toward the estimated 11 million people living illegally in the US. "Focusing on the border is increasingly missing the point in terms of immigration enforcement," Professor DeSipio says. "Those resources could have, in the Bush years particularly, been better balanced between border enforcement and interior enforcement."

The situation today calls for a nuanced approach to enforcement that considers the significant number of people who enter the country legally and overstay their visas, says Bingel of Command Consulting Group.

"In some ways the debate needs to shift a bit to think of it more like you think of crime statistics in a city," he adds. "You wouldn't say that the police force is ineffective in a major metropolitan area unless there [is] zero crime. And you have to apply similar thinking to the border."

Ms. Vaughan of the Center for Immigration Studies acknowledges that fresh thinking is needed. She says the government should waive some environmental regulations that prevent border patrol agents from accessing some lands. She says officials should focus interdiction efforts not just on highways, but also on bus stations and airports. And she agrees that the US needs to look inward.

"We're reaching a point where we are much closer to operational control now, but it's really in interior enforcement where we need to pick up the pace so that it takes off some of the pressures at the physical border," she says.

Critical Thinking

1. How can the challenges of illegal immigration be met?
2. How will a beefed up border patrol deter new illegal border crossings?

Create Central

www.mhhe.com/createcentral

Internet References

http://heritageaction.com/2013/06/secret-amendment-takes-resources-from-southern-border

www.cato.org/sites/cato.org/files/serials/files/cato-journal/2012/1/cj32n1-8.pdf

www.dispatch.com/content/stories/national_world/2013/06/21/plan-calls-for-fortifying-southern-border.html

www.policymic.com/articles/24236/immigration-reform-2013-why-is-amnesty-such-a-dirty-word

www.weeklystandard.com/articles/amnesty-next-time_722057.html

Article

Prepared by: Sudip Ghosh, *Penn State University—Berks*

Panic Over US Tapering, China Growth Overdone, Insists IIF

Leading Economists have Urged Latin American Policymakers not to Abandon the Economic Reforms.

THIERRY OGIER, LUCIEN CHAUVIN, AND JENNY LOWE

Learning Outcomes

After reading this article, you will be able to:

- Understand the emerging market in Latin America.

- Understand economic reform.

- Identify the "fragile five."

Amid fears of a perfect storm of spiking US rates and a sharp Chinese slowdown breaking over the region, leading economists have urged Latin American policymakers not to abandon the economic reforms that have so far kept the region from recession.

However they insisted countries would remain under pressure this year as the looming monetary tightening in the US and the China-related soft commodity prices acted as a drag.

The Institute of International Finance (IIF) said that sound economic policy was the solution. "This is not rocket science," said Ramon Aracena, its chief Latin America economist. "The recipes are here. Do your homework and you will see that the possibility of contagion is more limited because people trust you."

The IIF said economic expansion was likely to decelerate to 2.1 percent this year compared to 2.4 percent in 2013. In 2015, the positive impact of Mexico's reforms and a recovery in Brazil should help push the regional average to 2.7 percent.

Rodrigo Vergara, central bank governor of Chile, said the region would probably grow less this year than last year. "Mexico and Brazil together add up to 62 percent of the region's GDP. It is not only that they affect the weighted average with their slower growth, but they also are where many of the countries in the region can export manufactured goods."

However, Charles Collyns, managing director and chief economist of the IIF, insisted that the US/China double-whammy was not likely to result in a substantial capital flight. "Pessimism is overdone," he said in an interview with Emerging Markets. "We think there is a reasonable outlook for stabilization of capital flows in emerging markets, including in Latin America. In fact there has been a gradual increase lately.

"Capital has continued to flow in a positive direction toward capital markets. There has been a pick-up in February and March. We think that this trend can continue."

The macroeconomic situation has remained unstable in some countries like Argentina and Venezuela, but most Latin American policymakers have achieved a good level of credibility, including Brazil's central bank, according to Collyns who added that other countries had "gaps in their policy framework."

He said the China slowdown would have a greater negative impact on exporting countries than US monetary policy. A combination of both would harm Brazil, Chile, and Peru, he said.

China has several problems to solve including credit growth, the shadow banking system, and signs of overheating in various sectors that may lead to restrictive measures, which in turn may affect Latin America, according to the Mexican deputy governor of the central bank Manuel Sanchez.

Craig Botham, emerging markets economist at Schroders, said Brazil and the other members of the so-called fragile five group of emerging markets had made the adjustments needed to reduce current account deficits.

He said that the situation was less worrying than six months ago but added: "They are still dependent on these flows. They are balancing a big chunk of economic activity through foreign money and that foreign money is about to get more expensive and hurt activity."

Nicolas Cowley, Henderson Global Investors' head of Latin American equities, said the markets had got used to the impact of the tapering of US quantitative easing.

"It is a headwind for EM for the next couple of years, but it is perhaps better understood by investors because it has gone from an unknown impact to us seeing how it affects the economy and it really isn't as bad as people initially feared," he said.

Peru Economy and Finance Minister Luis Miguel Castilla said there had been a "normalization of the conditions in the world. The major hit was taken around a year ago, when the announcement that tapering would start was made. A rebalancing has been going on that has already been internalized by market."

So far GDP growth has been somewhat disappointing. Enrique Garcia, president of CAF, said Latin American would grow by around 3 percent this year, but should in fact grow by twice as much.

Critical Thinking

1. Explain how the Chinese slowdown will impact Latin American growth.
2. Why should economic reform be in place in Latin American countries to challenge slowdown in China?
3. What are some of the challenges faced by Latin American nations as a whole?

Create Central

www.mhhe.com/createcentral

Internet References

Real Clear World

http://www.realclearworld.com/articles/2013/08/23/how_chinas_slowdown_will_impact_latin_america_105397.html

Truthout

http://www.truth-out.org/news/item/24209-china-trades-up-in-latin-america

Zunia

http://zunia.org/post/how-would-a-chinese-slowdown-affect-latin-america

Ogier, Thierry; Chauvin, Lucien; and Lowe, Jenny. From *Emerging Markets Magazine*, March 29, 2014. Copyright © 2014 Emerging Markets Newspaper. Reprinted with permission.

Article

Prepared by: Sudip Ghosh, *Penn State University—Berks*

Weakly Capitalized Banks Slowed Lending Recovery After Recession

J.B. COOKE AND CHRISTOFFER KOCH

Learning Outcomes

After reading this article, you will be able to:

• Understand the relationship between bank capital and lending.

• Identify the channels of monetary policy.

• Discuss credit growth trends.

Commercial banks, credit unions, and savings and loans sustained substantial losses during the Great Recession and ensuing financial crisis, exemplified by a 7.4-percent delinquency rate for U.S. commercial banks' total loans and leases in first quarter 2010.[1]

Real estate was especially weak, with residential loan delinquencies peaking at 11.3 percent in the first quarter of 2010 and commercial real estate delinquencies at 8.8 percent a quarter later. Also, high by historical standards was the 4.3 percent delinquency rate for commercial and industrial loans in third quarter 2009.[2]

The resulting loan losses ate into bank capital, the first line of defense for large depositors and debt holders, boosting the institutions' leverage. A simultaneous decline in wholesale funding—via commercial paper or large time-deposits, for example—reduced the supply of loans, according to the Federal Reserve Senior Loan Officers' Opinion Survey. This slowdown occurred even though Fed monetary policy was highly accommodative in a concerted effort to stimulate economic growth.[3]

The reluctance to lend played out particularly among a subset of banks—often larger institutions with very low ratios of capital to assets.[4] If these institutions had behaved as the other banks did, the cumulative amount of loan activity might have been 5.8 percent higher during 2009–2010, our analysis indicates—and might have provided greater support to Fed recovery efforts.

Channels of Monetary Policy

Monetary policy ripples through the economy via various transmission channels, including the *price* and *quantity channels*.

The price channel (the cost of or interest rate for borrowed funds) can affect the timing of consumer spending and investment. By contrast, the quantity channel operates through the balance sheets of households, businesses, and banks and other financial intermediaries such as savings and loans (also called thrifts) and credit unions. Their levels of indebtedness affect both the amount and cost of borrowing. Among depository financial institutions, the quantity channel is often referred to as the *lending channel*.[5]

An impaired balance sheet is one reason depositories' lending has been slow to recover since the financial crisis. Variations in lending activity can result from changes in loan demand and in the supply of loans. For example, loan demand declines during recessions and rises in recoveries. The supply of loans may fall if depositors or other creditors withdraw funding that banks may find difficult to replace, or if banks anticipate or incur large loan losses.

When loan losses occur, leverage rises—there is less equity standing behind outstanding loans—and lending standards tend to tighten.

Capitalization Matters

Overall commercial bank deposit growth slowed markedly, from an average year-over-year rate of 8.4 percent in

2000–2008 to 5.8 percent in 2009–2010. Growth dipped to a low of 2.3 percent in December 2010 as hard-pressed households drew down their savings. Large time-deposits shrank by an average annual rate of 6.4 percent from October 2008 to December 2010 after growing an average 12.7 percent from 2000 to September 2008.

Large loan losses during the economic downturn eroded institutions' capital and may have scared away some large depositors and creditors.

Because capital helps protect large debt holders, it is instructive to look at the lending behavior of banks with differing ratios of capital to assets to see how lending in 2009–2010 was affected at banks with lower capital ratios. Many of these institutions engaged in earlier, boom-period risk taking and credit growth.

Academic research on the lending channel has focused almost exclusively on commercial banks.[6] Evidence suggests that the lending channel works primarily through those commercial banks that are more likely to be financially constrained. Illiquidity, small asset size and low capitalization can serve as proxies for the limitations confronting these institutions.[7]

Asset size and capitalization are negatively correlated for commercial banks, credit unions and savings and loans. Although the number of all three types of depositories has fallen steadily over time, the relative market shares of commercial banks, credit unions and thrifts by asset size did not fundamentally change between 2000 and 2012. In the fourth quarter 2008, for example, it's clear that banks were among the largest institutions (*Chart 1*).[8]

Commercial banks account for about 86 percent of lending, followed by credit unions, and savings and loans at 7 percent each. Credit unions are the most common type of small- to medium-sized depository.

Large institutions tend to have lower capital ratios.

Credit Growth Trends

Commercial banks experienced strong lending growth during the boom years after the 2001 recession, peaking at 9.2 percent in the third quarter 2004 (*Chart 2*).[9]

Credit growth among banks ebbed notably during the recovery, and in the second quarter 2011, lending contracted 1.8 percent. Thrifts also experienced substantial lending growth during the boom years, gaining 8.5 percent in the second quarter 2006 before declining 3.2 percent in the first quarter 2011. Credit unions did not expand their lending as much during the boom period, topping out at 5.4 percent in first quarter 2006 before contracting 2.4 percent in first quarter 2011.

Part of the difference in the lending dynamics of banks, thrifts, and credit unions is explained by the composition of their loan portfolios and resulting business-cycle sensitivity. For instance, compared with banks or thrifts, credit unions grant few commercial and industrial, construction and development, and commercial real estate loans. They predominantly make residential mortgage, auto and other consumer loans.[10]

However, portfolio composition does not fully explain why lending patterns of the least-capitalized banks and thrifts differed greatly from their better-capitalized counterparts.

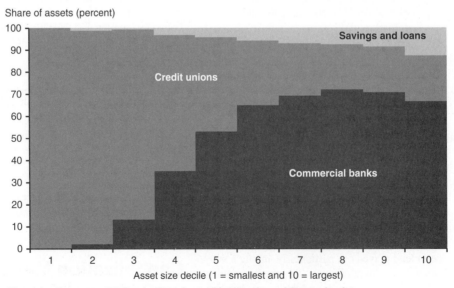

Chart 1   Commercial Banks Dominate Distribution of Depositories

Note: Data are for the fourth quarter 2008.

Sources: Reports of Condition and Income; Federal Financial Institutions Examination Council; authors' calculations.

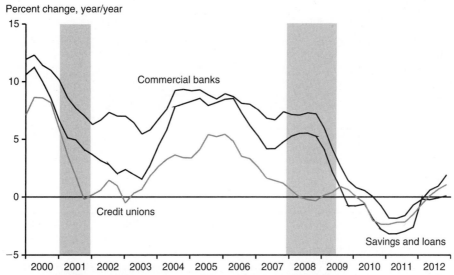

Percent change, year/year

Chart 2   Median Lending Growth Slowly Recovers from Recession

Note: Shaded areas represent recessions.

Sources: Reports of Condition and Income; Federal Financial Institutions Examination Council; authors' calculations.

The origins of weak overall lending growth are evident in institutions' level of capitalization. The three panels in *Chart 3* display year-over-year median lending growth by capitalization decile (from weakest/lowest to strongest/highest) according to institution type.[11]

The difference in the lending growth of the least-capitalized (red line) and better-capitalized commercial banks and thrifts is apparent. During the sluggish 2009–2010 recovery, credit largely contracted among the weaker, least-capitalized banks and thrifts. Because capitalization is negatively correlated with institution size, the large, highly leveraged banks and thrifts followed a softer lending growth path, impacting overall credit growth.

If lending at the least-capitalized commercial banks had grown at the same rate it did at the other 90 percent of commercial banks, cumulative credit expansion might have been 1 percent lower during the lending boom's peak (second quarter 2003 to second quarter 2005)—and 5.8 percent higher during the lending collapse (fourth quarter 2008 to fourth quarter 2010).[12] In other words, monetary easing would have more effectively supported the economy through the lending channel during the recovery if the most leveraged (predominantly large) banks had held more capital.

A similar conclusion applies to thrifts and credit unions. Quantitatively, the low-capitalization effect is more pronounced for thrifts; for credit unions, it's only about half of that exhibited by banks. Overall, if the lending growth of the least-capitalized commercial banks, thrifts, and credit unions equaled the rate

of the other 90 percent of depositories, cumulative lending in 2009–2010 would have been 5.5 percent higher.

Diminishing Drag on Lending

Low capitalization was a problem for a subset of highly leveraged commercial banks and thrifts during the 2009–2010 recovery. Because the highly leveraged banks and thrifts tended to be larger, they dragged down aggregate credit growth. The lending paths of the least- and most-capitalized credit unions were similar.

In the past couple of years, lending growth at the least-capitalized commercial banks and thrifts has slowly picked up, although not yet at the rate of their better-capitalized counterparts. This growth signals not only that the U.S. economy is continuing to rebound from the Great Recession and financial crisis, but also that some of the weaker links in the financial system are on their way to recovery.

Notes

1. Delinquent loans include those past due 30 days or more and still accruing interest, as well as those more in arrears that are on nonaccrual status.

2. The overall delinquency rate was 2.7 percent from the first quarter 1991 to the fourth quarter 2007. The rates were 2.2 percent for residential loans, 3.5 percent for commercial real estate loans, and 2.6 percent for commercial and industrial loans.

A. Commercial Banks
Growth (percent)

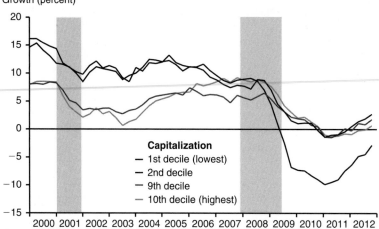

B. Credit Unions
Growth (percent)

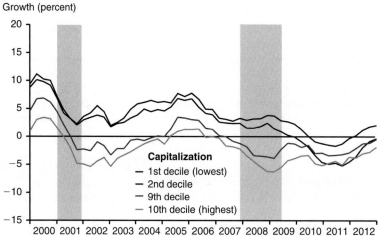

C. Savings and Loans
Growth (percent)

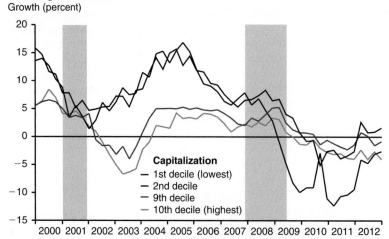

Chart 3   Capitalization Levels Affect Willingness to Lend (Median year/year lending growth by depository type)

Note: Shaded areas represent recessions.

Sources: Reports of Condition and Income; Federal Financial Institutions Examination Council; authors' calculations.

3. The Federal Reserve, in line with its mandate, supported the economic recovery by lowering the federal funds rate, engaging in large-scale asset purchases and providing forward guidance regarding the evolution of the federal funds rate.

4. A bank's portfolio of loans is the principal asset on an institution's balance sheet.

5. Note that these transmission channels are not mutually exclusive and may interact in a number of ways. More extensive reviews of monetary transmission channels can be found in textbooks such as *Monetary Theory and Policy,* by Carl E. Walsh, Cambridge, Mass.: MIT Press, 2010.

6. For example, see "What Do a Million Observations on Banks Have to Say About the Monetary Transmission Mechanism?" by Anil K. Kashyap and Jeremy C. Stein, *American Economic Review,* vol. 90, no. 3, 2000, pp. 407–28; "Bank Size, Bank Capital, and the Bank Lending Channel," by R.P. Kishan and T.P. Opiela, *Journal of Money, Credit and Banking,* vol. 32, no. 1, 2000, pp. 121–41; and "New Evidence on the Lending Channel," by A.B. Ashcraft, *Journal of Money, Credit and Banking,* vol. 38, no. 3, 2006, pp. 751–75.

7. See note 6. Kashyap and Stein emphasize illiquidity and size, Kishan and Opiela capitalization.

8. A large part of the decline in numbers was driven by mergers rather than outright failures. The depositories are sorted by asset size from smallest to largest and then divided into 10 equal-sized groups. The first group, or decile, represents the smallest institutions; the 10th decile contains the largest ones.

9. The median is less influenced by outliers than the mean (simple average), and year-over-year changes are not affected by seasonality in lending.

10. The uptick in credit union lending toward the end of the Great Recession may reflect the cash-for-clunkers federal program that disproportionately affected depositories with a larger share of consumer loans. The first-time homebuyer tax credit likely played a part in thrifts' brief lending rise in 2010.

11. Capitalization could be measured using a risk-weighted capital ratio instead of the simple capital-to-total-assets ratio. However, simple measures of capitalization convey much the same information as more complex ones, as Michael A. Seamans points out in "When Gauging Bank Capital Adequacy: Simplicity Beats Complexity," Federal Reserve Bank of Dallas *Economic Letter,* vol. 8, no. 2, 2013.

12. These results were generated from a fixed-effects-panel data regression. Lending growth was regressed on time-fixed effects (FEs), capitalization, size, size $\times$ capitalization (interactions), time FEs $\times$ size, time FEs $\times$ capitalization. The time fixed effects capture aggregate macroeconomic factors. Capitalization is highly significant.

Critical Thinking

1. Why are banks refraining from lending?

2. What happens if banks reduce lending, and how can the Fed intervene?

3. How is credit tied to lending?

Create Central

www.mhhe.com/createcentral

Internet References

Social Science Research Network
   http://papers.ssrn.com/sol3/papers.cfm?abstract_id=2388773
Huffington Post
   www.huffingtonpost.com%2F2013%2F07%2F10%2Fbanks-capital-lending_n_3573704.html

Article   Prepared by: Sudip Ghosh, *Penn State University—Berks*

Immigration Reform Could Boost U.S. Economy

Immigration Bill could Put Economy into Overdrive.

Despite a lull in recent years, a Pew Research Center report suggests that illegal immigration rates are climbing in response to the recovering economy.

LAUREN FOX

Learning Outcomes

After reading this article, you will be able to:

- Discuss immigration reform.

- Understand how jobs are affected by immigration.

Opponents to immigration reform have called the Senate's bipartisan and comprehensive immigration reform bill a "job killer," but a new report by the conservative-leaning American Action Network, is evidence that the bill might just be the stimulus Congress has been looking for to put the stagnant economy into overdrive.

From California to South Carolina, the report shows that the Senate's immigration bill would create an average of 14,000 jobs per congressional district in the next decade.

Majority Whip Rep. Kevin McCarthy, R-Calif., a key member of the House leadership whose agricultural district is more than 30 percent Latino, would see nearly 17,000 new jobs back home if the Senate bill were implemented. And even Rep. Steve King, R-Iowa, who has made headlines for expressing disdain for immigrants who entered the country illegally, would see more than 13,000 new jobs in his district.

It is not the first to show that immigration reform could stimulate the economy. The Congressional Budget Office estimated the Senate bill would cut the deficit by more than $680 billion,

and a July study by the Institute on Taxation and Economic Policy showed that reform would boost state and local tax revenues by $2 billion a year.

In June, the Senate overwhelmingly passed the Border Security, Economic Opportunity, and Immigration Modernization Act of 2013 complete with its reformed visa programs and a path to citizenship for the 11 million immigrants who entered the country illegally. But Republican leaders within the House of Representatives have sworn off the bill as too progressive, expensive, and ineffective. They even blasted the border surge plan, which would double the number of border patrol agents.

House Speaker John Boehner has stated he won't bring the Senate bill to floor, but will instead count on his committee leaders to work on legislation piece by piece. So far, the House has cleared border security bills from committee, but have not dealt with the question of what to do with immigrants living in the country illegally.

The American Action Network has spent $1 million fighting for immigration reform since March and is optimistic that their efforts and the report might push House Republicans to act more quickly when they return from recess. The AAN is part of a broader coalition of Republican think tanks and leaders pushing an economic argument for immigration reform and hoping to convince members on the fence that supporting comprehensive reform could help the government generate more revenue.

"These findings prove that conservative immigration reform would help local economies in every district in America. Congress should continue working on true methodical immigration reform to fix the broken border and help local economies grow," AAN leader Brian Walsh said in a statement.

Critical Thinking

1. How would immigration reform boost tax revenues as projected by the Congressional Budget Office?
2. How would building a wall impact immigration?

Create Central

www.mhhe.com/createcentral

Internet References

Institute on Taxation and Economic Policy
   http://www.itep.org/immigration/
ProCon.org
   http://immigration.procon.org/view.answers.php?questionID=000789
Think Progress
   http://thinkprogress.org/immigration/2014/04/15/3426680/tax-day-undocumented-immigrants-pay-taxes/

Article   Prepared by: Sudip Ghosh, *Penn State University—Berks*

Economic Shocks Reverberate in World of Interconnected Trade Ties

Matthieu Bussière, Alexander Chudik, and Giulia Sestieri

Learning Outcomes

After reading this article, you will be able to:

- Understand economic shocks.
- Discuss the effects of international trade flows on GDP.
- Understand vertical integration of production chains.

Renewed debate about currency wars and the question of global trade imbalances are part of a longer-running economic discussion about what drives a country's exports and imports.

More specifically, what determines international trade flows? As the world economy slowly recovers from the Great Recession and global trade flows remain weak, net trade contributions to domestic growth become more critical and the factors affecting exports and imports tend to become more intensely scrutinized.

Studies of the current account—the balance of goods and services traded internationally, plus net income from abroad and net cross-border transfer payments—have long emphasized the role of the exchange rate in adjusting to excessive current account surpluses and deficits. In the context of global imbalances, several efforts have been made to estimate the magnitude of the dollar depreciation needed to reduce the U.S. trade deficit, which reached around 6 percent of gross domestic product (GDP) in the year preceding the 2008 financial crisis.[1] However, it's also important to take into account the role of demand because its fluctuations at home and abroad can offset relative price movements.

Based on a global vector autoregression (GVAR) macroeconomic model of trade flows, it appears that world exports respond more to an unexpected event, or shock, affecting U.S. output than to a comparable unplanned event involving the dollar. Additionally, shocks abroad bring wide-ranging responses that tend to be felt among countries with strong trading relationships. A positive bump to German output would increase output and exports among other European economies. Surprisingly, perhaps, it would also increase exports and GDP in more distant countries such as Mexico. The effect of a positive shock to Chinese imports would be especially large among other Asian countries but less so in Europe.

Modeling Economic Spillovers

The multilateral nature of international trade deserves particular attention, given that trade is increasingly fragmented. For example, a slowdown in economic activity in country A affects not only its trading partner, country B, but also country B's trading partners, C and D. This is particularly true if B imports from C and D the components needed to produce the goods exported to A.

GVAR modeling, which looks at relationships among series of data over time and across countries, offers a convenient and flexible way to study international trade because it takes into account cross-country interdependencies.

The model can capture strong links between exports and imports that occur because of vertical integration of production chains—an exported finished product includes imported components, for example. As a result, the model can look at global trade flows and the effect of unanticipated changes to variables such as aggregate demand—proxied here by GDP—and exchange rates.[2] These shocks may be correlated and may differ from the independent, economically unrelated shocks depicted in the so-called structural macroeconomic models.[3]

The trade model covers 21 countries—14 advanced and 7 emerging markets. The modeling strategy uses a handful of key variables: exports and imports of goods and services, GDP, effective exchange rates, and oil prices (all in real, or inflation-adjusted, terms), plus country-specific foreign data aggregates. These foreign aggregates are constructed as weighted cross-section averages of exports, imports, output, and exchange rates.

Data cover 1980 to 2007, an endpoint just before the onset of the Great Recession and ensuing trade collapse.

Unanticipated Rise in U.S. Output

Consider a positive shock to domestic output in the U.S., an unexpected/unpredictable rise in GDP over the period covered in the data sample. In the model, a one-standard-error shock to U.S. output—a size considered statistically typical—is equal to 0.6 percent of GDP at the time of impact. One noticeable result is a large effect on U.S. imports, which increase around 2 percent after one year and 1.3 percent after three years. In addition, the impact on other countries is significant and large.

Unsurprisingly, such a positive shock to U.S. output has expansionary effects on the output of almost all foreign countries (*Chart 1*). The squares in the chart represent the mean effect after one year, while the length of the associated bars indicates the degree of statistical uncertainty around the estimates. Although the effect is particularly large in neighboring Canada and Mexico, European economies are significantly affected, too, especially the smaller ones. The effect is positive but not statistically different from zero in several Asian countries, especially larger ones such as China and Japan.

Similarly, exports increase significantly in almost all countries (*Chart 2*). The effects of higher growth abroad generate a rise in U.S. exports. The positive feedback to U.S. exports is statistically and economically significant in the first couple of years after the shock.

The rankings of countries in *Charts 1* and *2* are similar, suggesting that geographic proximity and trade linkages are important channels of transmission. The model is symmetric—when an increase in U.S. output causes a substantial export increase, it follows that a U.S. recession would likely be associated with a significant fall in world trade.

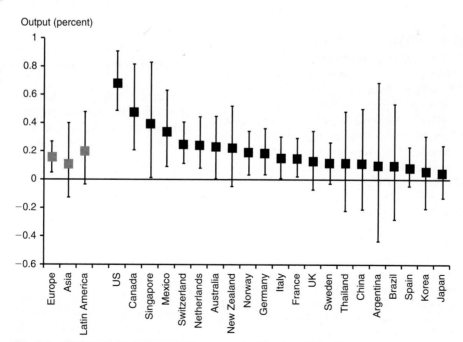

Chart 1　Global Output Rises in Response to Shock to U.S. Output

Note: Chart shows the impact of a U.S. output shock on global output after one year, with 90 percent confidence bounds.

Source: Authors' calculations.

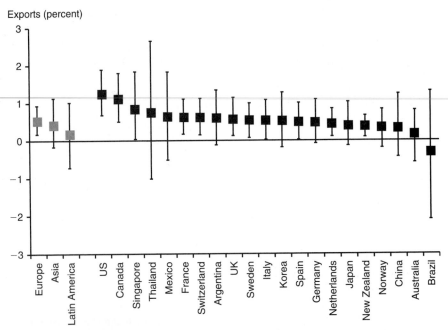

Chart 2 Global Exports Increase as U.S. Output Rises

Note: Chart shows the impact of a U.S. output shock on exports after one year, with 90 percent confidence bounds.

Source: Authors' calculations.

U.S. Dollar Appreciation

Next, suppose a positive shock occurs to the U.S. real effective exchange rate, which corresponds to an appreciation of 2.5 percent on impact.[4] The stronger dollar has an unambiguous effect on U.S. exports, which fall 1.3 percent in the first year (*Chart 3*).[5]

Japanese exports are affected by the U.S. exchange rate appreciation more than those of other foreign economies, in line with Japan experiencing the greatest resulting currency depreciation.[6] The stronger dollar also significantly affects exports from European countries. The overall effect on Asian and Latin American exports tends to be subdued. A possible explanation: the currencies of these regions tend to follow U.S. exchange-rate appreciation and gain little competitiveness when the dollar strengthens.

Thus, world exports respond more to a U.S. output shock than to a shock involving dollar appreciation. This appears to be consistent with what occurred after the 2008 financial crisis, when, contrary to what many observers expected, adjustment to global imbalances was not accompanied by a sharp dollar depreciation.

Other Country Shocks

Although the U.S. clearly has a leading role in the global business cycle, other countries play important roles. Accordingly, it is interesting to look at Germany and China to illustrate regional and global dynamics. Both countries are systemically important to the global economy and are forces in their own regions.

Germany is the world's fourth-largest economy and the foremost one in the euro area, as well as the second-largest global exporter after China. A positive, one-standard-deviation shock to German GDP, corresponding to a 0.8 percent increase at the time of impact, has a broad impact on exports after one year and carries economically and statistically significant effects on other countries, especially in Europe (*Chart 4*). This is not surprising given the strength of linkages in Europe. Interestingly, the effect on U.S. exports is also significant, at about 0.4 percent.

Finally, consider the effect on exports from a positive shock to Chinese imports, given the increasing importance of China in global trade (*Chart 5*). Although some of the estimated effects are uncertain, the general pattern is relatively clear: a one-standard-error shock to Chinese imports, which corresponds to an increase of 1.9 percent at the time of the impact, has a large positive effect on exports from other Asian countries and, to a lesser extent, exports from Europe after one year. This result clearly suggests the presence of strong trade integration among Asian economies.[7]

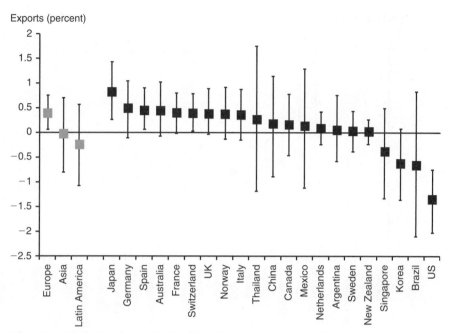

Chart 3   U.S. Dollar Appreciation Felt Most in Japan and Europe

Note: Chart shows the impact of a U.S. dollar shock on exports after one year, with 90 percent confidence bounds.

Source: Authors' calculations.

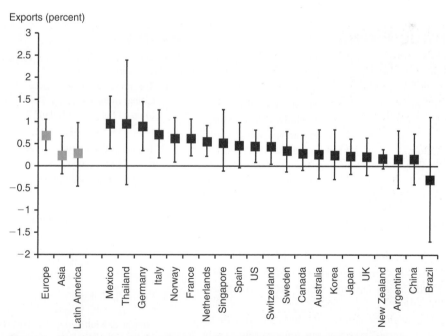

Chart 4   Response to Rising German Output Most Widely Felt in Europe

Note: Chart shows the impact of a German output shock on exports after one year, with 90 percent confidence bounds.

Source: Authors' calculations.

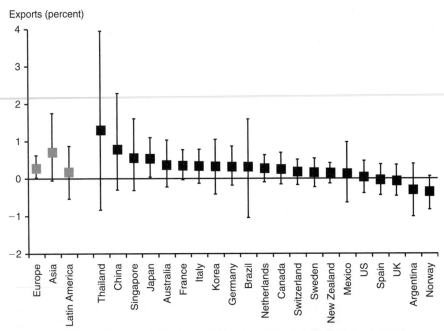

Chart 5   Global Exports Respond to Unexpected Rise in Chinese Imports

Note: Chart shows the impact of a Chinese import shock on exports after one year, with 90 percent confidence bounds.

Source: Authors' calculations.

Global Trade Flows

GVAR trade modeling, helpful in showing cross-country interdependence, suggests that changes in domestic demand have a strong effect on international trade flows and on foreign GDP. This underlines the importance of policy coordination across countries: in a strongly interconnected world in which economic shocks reverberate through international trade linkages, international spillover effects cannot be ignored. Policy measures in a given country affect its trading partners directly, and the effects quickly spread to the rest of the world, ultimately feeding back to the domestic economy itself.

The G-20, representing the largest and some of the most influential economies, offers a natural forum for policy coordination among systemically important countries.[8] This is particularly true of the G-20 working group on the Framework for Strong, Sustainable, and Balanced Growth, which seeks to address global imbalances.

Rebalancing the world economy—for instance, by stimulating demand in countries experiencing trade surpluses—is important to ensure that global growth does not rely on a small number of countries, each susceptible to downturns, but instead becomes more evenly spread among all nations.

Notes

Thanks to Bruno Cabrillac and Annabelle Mourougane for helpful comments and suggestions.

1. See, for example, the survey "A Framework for Assessing Global Imbalances," by Thierry Bracke, Matthieu Bussière, Michael Fidora and Roland Straub, *The World Economy,* vol. 33, no. 9, 2009, pp. 1,140–74 and the references cited therein.

2. Technically, the GVAR approach consists of estimating a set of small-scale country-specific dynamic models, which link domestic and foreign variables. The GVAR formulation is a rich dynamic model, which also allows for cointegration within and across countries. See "Modeling Global Trade Flows: results from a GVAR Model," by Matthieu Bussière, Alexander Chudik and Giulia Sestieri, Globalization and Monetary Policy Institute Working Paper no. 119, Federal Reserve Bank of Dallas, 2012, for details of the GVAR model used to generate these results and for a complete description of the data.

3. Generalized impulse response functions (GIRF) reported here (and originally proposed in "Impulse Response Analysis in Nonlinear Multivariate Models," by Gary Koop, M. Hashem Pesaran and Simon M. Potter, *Journal of Econometrics,* vol. 74, no. 1, 1996, pp. 119–47) give a sense of the expected impact of a change in one variable (demand or exchange rates) on other variables (trade flows) in the model.

Economic Shocks Reverberate in World of Interconnected Trade Ties by Matthieu Bussiere, Alexander Chudik, and Giulia Sestieri

87

4. The real effective exchange rate of the dollar is a weighted average value of the dollar relative to an index or basket of other major currencies, adjusted for the effects of inflation.

5. Preliminary results imply that a 10 percent appreciation of the dollar would trigger a more than 5 percent decline in U.S. real exports, which appears to be on the high side. Other researchers also find substantial effects (see, for example, "The New OECD International Trade Model," by Nigel Pain, Annabelle Mourougane, Franck Sédillot and Laurence Le Fouler, OECD Economics Department Working Papers no. 440, 2005, or "Trade Elasticities for the G-7 Countries," by Peter Hooper, Karen Johnson and Jaime Marquez, International Finance Discussion Paper no. 119, Federal Reserve Board of Governors, 1998. These comparisons are not without caveats because they refer to different definitions of relative prices and different country and time samples.

6. See note 2 (Figure 2).

7. Many papers have documented the increase in vertical specialization—the international fragmentation of production—and its important role in international transmission of business cycles. See, for example, "The Nature and Growth of Vertical Specialization in World Trade," by David Hummels, Jun Ishii and Kei-Mu Yi, *Journal of International Economics,* vol. 54, no. 1, 2001, pp. 75–96.

8. G-20 participants are Argentina, Australia, Brazil, Canada, China, France, Germany, India, Indonesia, Italy, Japan, Korea (Republic of), Mexico, Russia, Saudi Arabia, South Africa, Turkey, the U.K., and the U.S. in addition to the European Union.

Critical Thinking

1. How is global trade closely connected?

2. What effects do economic shocks have on global trade?

3. How does the U.S. dollar appreciation impact trade balance?

Create Central

www.mhhe.com/createcentral

Internet References

Voxeu
UNITAR
    http://www.voxeu.org/article/trade-policy-and-macroeconomic-shocks-new-evidence-emerging-economies
US News
    http://www.usnews.com/topics/subjects/international-trade

Article   Prepared by: Sudip Ghosh, *Penn State University—Berks*

RPT-Obamacare Is on the Horizon, but Will Enough People Sign Up?

DAVID MORGAN

Learning Outcomes

After reading this article, you will be able to:

• Understand the challenges facing Obamacare and the role of the government in boosting its enrollment.

• Explain why Obamacare will have fewer participants than anticipated.

Healthcare reform should be the signature Democratic achievement of President Barack Obama's presidency. But with "Obamacare" five months from show time, Democrats are worried about whether enough Americans will sign up to make the sweeping healthcare overhaul a success—and what failure might mean for Congress heading into the 2016 presidential race.

Some of the law's main advocates fear that not enough of America's 49 million uninsured will know about health coverage offered in their own states. Even if they do, new insurance plans may not be attractive to young, healthy consumers needed to offset an expected influx of older and sicker patients.

Only a handful of states are beginning campaigns to promote the online health insurance marketplaces created by the law. Known as exchanges, the markets will offer private coverage at federally subsidized rates to individuals and families with low-to-moderate incomes, with enrollment set to begin Oct. 1.

The federal government has kept quiet about its promotion plans, which are expected to begin in earnest over the summer.

While Obama and his administration say they are working nonstop on reform, analysts believe a poor performance could make the Patient Protection and Affordable Care Act a big enough campaign issue in 2014 to jeopardize Democratic control of the Senate—particularly if insurance costs rise sharply.

"There is reason to be very concerned about what's going to happen with young people. If their (insurance) premiums shoot up, I can tell you, that is going to wash into the United States Senate in a hurry," said Senator Ron Wyden, an Oregon Democrat.

Some Democrats are frustrated about the lack of details surrounding administration plans to promote the exchanges.

Senator Max Baucus, a chief architect of the reform law, said federal outreach efforts deserve a failing grade so far and could be heading for a "huge train wreck." He criticized Health and Human Services Secretary Kathleen Sebelius for the scant information her department has provided.

Funding Embargo

"Why in late April can't they show us any of what they've got planned? The rollout plan should already be in existence," an exasperated Democratic Senate aide said separately.

The law is expected to cover 15 million Americans next year through the exchanges and an expansion of Medicaid. The overall number is forecast to jump to 38 million by 2022.

Reform is facing challenges on several fronts. Big insurers appear wary of participating, raising questions about how competitive the exchanges will be. Businesses are mounting a new legal effort to stop the use of federal subsidies in exchanges run by Washington. And most states have balked at the exchanges and the Medicaid expansion.

Meanwhile, the enrollment effort is under threat from months of delay, a congressional Republican embargo on new funding and worries about how affordable the new plans will be, according to analysts, lawmakers, congressional aides, and former officials.

"I don't see how what they're planning to do is going to be adequate. The resources are too limited, the (law's) penalties are too weak and elite opposition in much of the country will undermine" enrollment, said Paul Starr, a Princeton professor and former health adviser to President Bill Clinton.

Add to that the challenge of reaching a public that is highly skeptical and often misinformed about the most complex social legislation since Medicare and Medicaid in the mid-1960s.

A Kaiser Family Foundation poll found that 77 percent of Americans know little or nothing about exchanges, while 40 percent erroneously think reforms create a government panel to make end-of-life decisions for people on Medicare.

An April survey of 1,003 people by HealthPocket, an online company that helps consumers find insurance, also found that the law's penalty for not buying coverage would not induce most 25-to-34-year-olds or 18-to-24-year-olds to purchase it.

Glitches and Bumps

Obama this week defended the pace of implementation, telling reporters that the government was working hard to "make sure that we're hitting all the deadlines and the benchmarks" even with the challenge of building the new online exchanges.

"That's still a big, complicated piece of business," Obama said, adding the task was made harder by a dedicated Republican opposition still determined to block the law's implementation.

"Even if we do everything perfectly, there'll still be, you know, glitches and bumps," he said.

The administration is building exchanges in 33 states that are unwilling or unable to do so on their own, and has limited funds for marketing. The remaining 17 states are building their own and have received sizable budgets for outreach.

Among states taking the lead, Vermont has launched radio advertising to raise public awareness. Colorado begins its public outreach this month, while California, Maryland, and the District of Columbia will hold off until later in the year.

For the federal exchanges, HHS has a contract worth at least $8 million with public relations firm Weber Shandwick and $54 million to train and pay "navigators," or counselors who will help consumers choose a health plan. It also has a $28 million contract with General Dynamics to set up a call center and will make its Healthcare.gov website consumer-oriented.

The administration is seeking help from major U.S. insurance providers to market aggressively to consumers on the federally run exchanges and help convince healthy citizens between 26 and 45 to pay for insurance instead of a first-year penalty amounting to $95 per person or 1 percent of household income.

Blowing Up

But reform advocates worry that the HHS budget is too small and the spigot for new funding from Congress is shut off by partisan politics. The "navigator" program allocates just $600,000 each for 13 states including Delaware, Iowa, Kansas, and New Hampshire.

"There's a limited amount of money that should be increased. But that's subject to appropriations and Congress is not likely to appropriate additional money," said Ron Pollack of the advocacy group Families USA. "It's going to require a very robust effort in the private sector."

Analysts say reform could be as big an issue in next year's congressional midterm elections as it was in 2010, when dislike for the law among senior citizens helped install a Republican majority in the House of Representatives. This time, failed implementation could end Democratic hopes of recapturing the House and leave enough Senate Democrats vulnerable to give Republicans an edge in that chamber.

"We have to see how bad it is. This issue blowing up on Democrats would make the Republicans' job a lot easier," said Jennifer Duffy of the Cook Political Report.

But Democrats believe implementation will also provide favorable coverage of deserving individuals and families finally being able to secure adequate and affordable health coverage after a long sojourn through the current marketplace.

There has been encouraging news for consumers. Vermont says 2014 premium rates will save money for residents. A family of four with an annual income of $75,000 would pay less than $600 per month for coverage with a federal subsidy, versus $900 for the cheapest small group plan available today.

Critical Thinking

1. How can Obamacare succeed?
2. Explain why Obamacare will face moral hazard issues and what the government can do to make it work.
3. Explain how Obamacare advocates can engage the consumer.

Create Central

www.mhhe.com/createcentral

Internet References

www.pbs.org/newshour/rundown/2013/04/top-five-ways-the-presidents-budget-would-change-medicare.html

www.foxnews.com/politics/2013/06/14/coverage-may-be-unaffordable-for-low-wage-workers-under-obamacare

www.forbes.com/fdc/welcome_mjx.shtml

www.commentarymagazine.com/2013/06/27/obamacare-and-unintended-consequences

Article   Prepared by: Sudip Ghosh, *Penn State University—Berks*

Economy Will Benefit from Immigration Reform

ROBERT L. CARET AND PAUL GUZZI

Learning Outcomes

After reading this article, you will be able to:

• Understand skilled worker immigration reforms.

• Discuss immigration reform.

Written off as dead, real immigration reform is back on the agenda in Washington—good news for American universities, American businesses and all of us who want to accelerate our slow economic recovery.

President Obama reaffirmed his commitment to immigration reform in his State of the Union address—and Republican leaders have expressed a willingness to work toward a successful bill. It may be that leaders of both parties have heard a loud and clear call over the last few months from business and higher education that we need the energy and intellect that constructive immigration reform can unleash if we are to remain competitive in the world economy.

In 2012–2013, more than 819,000 international students studied in the U.S.—3.9 percent of the total student population, contributing more than $24 billion to the U.S. economy. In many states, including Massachusetts, international students make up more than 5 percent of the student population. At the University of Massachusetts, 4,423 students—6.25 percent of total enrollment—were international in 2012. Most were degree-seeking graduate or doctoral students studying business administration, electrical and computer engineering, computer science, and chemistry and about half were citizens of China and India. For example, at the UMass flagship campus in Amherst, nearly 25 percent of graduate students were international and 48 percent of the overall pool of graduate school applicants were international students.

UMass is not alone. Universities are magnets for talented immigrants, particularly in the innovation-rich fields of science, technology, engineering, and mathematics (STEM). These graduates are consistently among the most productive workers in our economy. Far from taking jobs from Americans, they spur the creation of new ones. Every foreign-born advanced degree graduate working in a STEM field creates 2.62 American jobs.

Unfortunately, U.S. immigration policies have failed to keep pace in an increasingly globalized 21st-century economy. Outdated policy restrictions have prevented international students with STEM degrees, from American universities, from transitioning into our workforce. We train the world's brightest minds, only to have those students compete against us because our immigration laws do not offer a viable path forward. The bottom line is that this country's innovation economy loses when international students are forced to take their skills, ideas, and future job growth elsewhere. Furthermore, similarly restrictive immigration policies shut out from our economy thousands of skilled foreign workers and entrepreneurs.

This is why the University of Massachusetts has joined with other universities to support federal immigration reform. Similarly, the Greater Boston Chamber is leading a national coalition of more than 60 regional Chambers of Commerce from across the country seeking to enact skilled worker immigration reforms. Higher education and business recognize there is too much at stake for our nation's long-term competitiveness to allow this critical issue to go unaddressed.

Last year, the Senate passed comprehensive immigration reform that dramatically improves our nation's ability to retain global talent. House leadership has indicated a new willingness to act. They must seize this historic opportunity to pass immigration reforms, particularly focusing on the following areas:

- **Graduates**—Increase the availability of permanent resident visas (green cards) for foreign students graduating from a U.S. university with an advanced degree in the STEM fields. A policy in which green cards are "stapled to the diplomas" of STEM graduates will help reverse the international brain drain of these highly educated young people. In addition, allowing dual intent for F-1 student visas would enable more employers to start the green card process while students are in school or a related training program.

- **Skilled Workers**—Increase the availability of temporary, skilled worker (H-1B) visas by substantially raising the annual cap and enabling market-based adjustments. Creating a streamlined, market-driven H-1B visa program will boost the competitiveness of our nation's healthcare, life science, technology, manufacturing, finance, and insurance industries. In addition, reallocating the fees collected from H1-B visas and STEM green cards to fund state-level STEM education and worker retraining programs could bolster the domestic skilled worker pipeline.

- **Entrepreneurs**—Create new startup visas for immigrant entrepreneurs who launch businesses here and meet key job creation, revenue generation, and financing goals. U.S. immigration law does not currently provide an entrepreneur visa—a policy gap increasingly out of

step with our economic competitors. Creating a new visa category will ensure that the U.S. remains a global center for startups and innovation for decades to come.

As a nation, we cannot afford to put off reforming our immigration system any longer. Our future success depends upon Washington acting collaboratively so that we can continue to attract and retain the world's smartest and most entrepreneurial students and workers.

Critical Thinking

1. Critically examine how economy benefits from immigration and discuss.

2. Why and how do higher education institutes believe that immigrants contribute to the economy in different ways?

Create Central

www.mhhe.com/createcentral

Internet References

American Council on Education
   http://www.acenet.edu/news-room/Pages/Immigration-Reform-Priorities-for-Higher-Education.aspx
The Chronicle of Higher Education
   http://chronicle.com/article/Immigration-Overhaul-Hailed/140055/
Diverse
   http://diverseeducation.com/article/57853/

Unit 5

UNIT

Prepared by: Sudip Ghosh, *Penn State University—Berks*

The Changing Global Economy

War-torn nation in parts of the Middle East coupled with political instability in other parts of the world a surge in illegal immigration in the United States, Western Europe, and other South Asian nations. This is quite challenging for those governments as they are not equipped to handle problems of illegal immigration.

However, illegal immigrants in the U.S. are actually helping the stagnant housing market, gentrifying neighborhood thus reducing crime. Based on that advocates of immigration are hoping that the current administration will give "Amnesty" to millions of undocumented workers who are already present in the U.S.

Bitcoin Only Worth What People Think It Is Worth by Brian Bru...

95

Article   Prepared by: Sudip Ghosh, *Penn State University—Berks*

Bitcoin Only Worth What People Think It Is Worth

BRIAN BRUS

Learning Outcomes

After reading this article, you will be able to:

- Understand fluctuation in bitcoins valuation.

- Understand fractional banking system.

D r. Keith Smith has been watching the rise and fall of the bitcoin digital currency with curiosity since the Surgery Center of Oklahoma decided last year to accept bitcoin transactions.

Bitcoin reflects his libertarian view of the free market, Smith said, and it's proven its viability since entering the mainstream in 2009 as an alternative to the government-controlled dollar. So the recent discovery that millions of bitcoins had been stolen from the online exchange Mt. Gox, damaging consumer confidence and devaluing the currency, isn't necessarily the end of the line.

"I don't think bitcoin will be the last cryptocurrency we see. And I think they'll benefit from the errors and mistakes currently being experienced with bitcoin."

By the end of business Thursday, the value of each bitcoin in circulation was about $590—that's in terms of U.S. currency—down about 3 percent for the day, according to CoinDesk.com. On January 6, a single bitcoin could be exchanged for $950.

When the Surgery Center does accept a bitcoin payment, it will immediately be exchanged for dollars, Smith said. The business has no intention to hold onto the currency as an investment. A bitcoin market crash would have a negligible impact, if any, on the Surgery Center's bookkeeping for the day.

Therein lies the paradox of bitcoin's value as a legitimate currency, economics professor Jonathan Willner said. The harsh truth is that bitcoin, like any other token medium of exchange,
is only worth what people believe it is worth. Smith's quick exchange would be smarter than holding bitcoins and trusting other people's sense of consistency.

But only barely.

"You can have disasters with currency systems with or without regulation and oversight," Willner said. "I believe the potential of a disaster is slightly greater, and only slightly, when the currency system is private or a cryptocurrency like bitcoin."

Bitcoin was established in 2009 by an unknown individual or group operating under a pseudonym. The system that was created doesn't rely on a central manager; the worldwide bitcoin ledger is maintained in a decentralized peer-to-peer network and verified with high-level, digital cryptography. All bitcoin transactions are saved publicly and permanently online, although user identities can still be hidden.

Each new economics student is taught that money has three attributes: it must store value, be a unit of account, and serve as a medium of exchange.

Chocolate bars and cigarettes can be used as currency within prison systems, for example. Until it's burned to a butt, a cigarette might change hands several times with the value of a particular favor or other known quantity of consumable goods.

"So it's really about confidence," Willner said. "You've got to believe that you can trade it in for something later. Confederate dollars after the Civil War? No longer useful, unless you're a collector."

Ron Powers at Oklahoma Coin, Gold & Silver said he isn't even interested in bitcoin as a novelty, and definitely not as a legitimate store of value. Because bitcoins are created electronically, they have no true physical form as coin or cash, although some companies have minted tokens imprinted with a bitcoin access code.

"A lot of people are scared of it right now. They don't understand it," Powers said. "The old standard money works for us."

Other numismatists such as Shawnee Maxwell, owner of Southwest Coin, Stamp & Jewelry agreed with Powers that recent bitcoin news is cause for caution. She doesn't like the lack of government regulation.

Willner said that contrary to bitcoin proponents, the virtual currency concept is not new—the Fed does most of its accounting electronically now anyway, and people have given up on walking around with gold in their pockets. For that matter, gold itself is only as valuable as a currency as society agrees it is.

Compounding the cryptocurrency problem, Willner said, bitcoin's founders and online exchanges are sidestepping something called fractional reserve banking. That's a practice in which banks retain reserves equal to a portion of customers' deposits in case a lot of people want to withdraw at once. The rest of the deposits can be loaned out to earn interest from other customers, but there's always an understanding that the money will ultimately be redeposited down the line in other accounts and loaned again. At each step, there's a possibility of a consumer run on the bank.

Without a breaking mechanism of fractional reserve banking imposed by a central bank, a unit of currency can quickly multiply across several accounts of virtual debt. Proponents of government-free finances are risking their savings in a Ponzi scheme that could collapse at any time, Willner said.

"But even with a strong central bank and oversight authority, it doesn't mean you're safe either," he said. "Zimbabwe happens. Israel happens. Germany in the 1920s happens. . . . And history has examples of bankers who print their own money and suddenly disappear. So you can have disasters in any case. You can't trust human behavior."

The bottom line is that bitcoin and other new cryptocurrencies may very well last for decades, Willner said. In the interim stricter oversight systems could be put in place to help avoid digital bank thefts and Ponzi crashes.

"Who watches the watchers is always going to be a problem," he said. "People don't have a sufficient understanding of banking history."

Critical Thinking

1. Why are bitcoins problematic?
2. What will make bitcoins viable as a medium of exchange?

Create Central

www.mhhe.com/createcentral

Internet References

The Economist
http://www.economist.com/topics/bitcoins

Huffington Post
http://www.huffingtonpost.com/news/bitcoins/

CNN Money
http://money.cnn.com/infographic/technology/what-is-bitcoin/

Article   Prepared by: Sudip Ghosh, *Penn State University - Berks*

Austerity on the Side: EU Hits Restaurateurs with Olive Oil Law

ROBERT BRIDGE

Learning Outcomes

After reading this article, you will be able to:

- Understand the challenges of austerity in EU nations.

- Learn how austerity is impacting the restaurant business in EU nations.

As if European Union bureaucrats don't have enough on their hands trying to extinguish financial fires raging across the broken continent, they've now decided to take their unlimited powers to the holy of holies: EU eateries.

Yes, at a time when harsh austerity measures, delayed retirements and high unemployment levels are pushing Europeans to vent their outrage on the cobblestone streets, Brussels decided this was the perfect time to impose strict new rules on how restaurants serve olive oil to their customers.

Starting January 1, 2014, eateries will be prohibited from serving olive oil to diners in the traditional glass jugs that have been adorning European tables since at least the Middle Ages. Instead, cafes, bistros and brasseries will be forced to provide their patrons with pre-sealed, non-refillable containers that cannot be easily recycled when empty.

Once upon a time, Europe set the standards on environmental issues; now, it is behaving no better than Little Jack Horner, sticking its dirty fingers where they don't belong. Yet it is trying to convince the world that it just wants to protect the health of the average EU diner, the same group of people that was physically and morally assaulted by raw austerity measures.

Remember a few months ago when the European Commission was busy disassembling the EU's world-class welfare system in order to pay back the interest on central bank loans needed to rescue the bankers—the same scoundrels who triggered the global financial crisis in the first place? At that time, Brussels didn't so much as bat an eyelid about the health and well being of their fellow Europeans.

Suddenly, however, EU ministers have decided to wage a war on bad hygiene and sound traditions when many Europeans can't afford a bar of decent soap. They also say the move will help reassure what's left of their consumer base that the olive oil found in EU restaurants has not been diluted with an inferior (Read: Less expensive) product.

No wonder that critics say the rules, aside from boosting profits of the biggest olive oil producing companies (small, private proprietors need not apply), will increase the frustration felt by many towards a Brussels bureaucracy machine that is already seen to be out of touch with the issues affecting ordinary Europeans.

"If the European Union was logical and properly run, people wouldn't be so anti-Europe," said Marina Yannakoudakis, a British Conservative member of the European Parliament, as quoted by Reuters. *"But when it comes up with crazy things like this, it quite rightly calls into question their legitimacy and judgment."*

Yannakoudakis said the new measures highlighted how out of touch Brussels' priorities are.

Ironically, the Eurozone countries worst affected by the euro crisis—Italy, Greece, Spain and Portugal—where unemployment levels are sky-high, are also the continent's largest olive oil producers. It remains to be seen how the new legislation will affect the small olive oil producers in those already pressed economies.

German newspaper *Sueddetsche Zeitung* called the plan *"the weirdest decision since the legendary curvy cucumber regulation"*, referring to former EU rules governing the shape of fruit and vegetables found in supermarkets.

Enzo Sica, owner of Italian restaurant Creche des Artistes close to the EU quarter of Brussels, said the rules would prevent him from buying his extra virgin olive oil direct from a traditional supplier in Italy.

"They say they're thinking about consumers, but this will increase costs for us and our customers as well," he told Reuters. *"In this time of crisis, surely they should be worrying about other things rather than stupid stuff like this."*

Although Brussels' olive oil ruling isn't quite as inflammatory as was Marie Antoinette's unfortunate quip, *"Let them eat cake,"* it does adequately show that EU ministers are dangerously out of touch with the real issues now affecting millions of people across the Eurozone.

Critical Thinking

1. Discuss how best to meet challenges of austerity.
2. Discuss how EU leaders are micromanaging restaurants in EU nations.

Create Central

www.mhhe.com/createcentral

Internet References

www.ft.com/cms/s/0/2559506a-de5e-11e2-b990-00144feab7de
.html#axzz2XWzvo5M4

www.ft.com/intl/indepth/austerity-in-europe

www.europeagainstausterity.org

ROBERT BRIDGE is the author of the book, *Midnight in the American Empire,* which discusses the dangers of extreme corporate power in the United States.

Article

Prepared by: Sudip Ghosh, *Penn State University—Berks*

Crowdfunding Diplomacy: the Next Frontier for Government

Daniella Foster

Learning Outcomes

After reading this article, you will be able to:

- Understand and define crowdfunding.

- Discuss alternative finance.

- Explain the role of crowdfunding.

A common mantra among entrepreneurs is that failure is good; the key is to fail fast and fail cheap. If you applied this mantra to diplomacy the objective would be to test new approaches, with the goal of positively impacting communities abroad and adding new tools to a diplomat's tool belt, all while leveraging limited resources and responding to increasing demands. The challenge is that trying something new requires risk, and risk is not a trait synonymous with government. How do you encourage innovation in government and mitigate risk? The answer: develop strategic partnerships with partners who know how to innovate and manage risk and who have built-in platforms and systems to do so.

One area ripe for this type of partnership is crowdfunding, an alternative form of finance where money can be raised online through a crowdfunding platform (CFP) from friends, family, extended networks, and—thanks to Title III of the Jobs Act passed last year—investors. Hailed as the democratization of finance, individuals, non-profits, and companies have turned to crowdfunding to fund new projects, engaging their networks in the process, and enabling the community to curate ideas and fund over $2.6 billion in 2012, according to Massolution's *2013CF Crowdfunding Market: Software and Solutions Report.*

If you combined government's ability to convene and accelerate projects globally with the crowdfunding platform's ability to engage local communities and investors in projects, you would have a potentially game-changing impact on grassroots diplomacy and development. Why? Because in an era of budget cuts, the value that government brings to the table has shifted from funder to partner. And crowdfunding provides the ultimate platform for government to convene partners in the private sector and civil society around locally driven solutions that need financing. The model of government as the primary funder for social good initiatives is evolving as public-private partnerships, where corporate or non-government partners bring their resources and expertise to the table, are stepping in to provide pro-bono technical assistance, infrastructure, distribution channels and training to help address complex challenges such as youth unemployment, access to education, and global health.

There are three ways government can test-drive crowdfunding (and see if the democratization of finance is all it is cracked up to be).

1. Crowdfund a government innovation fund

Savvy diplomats have started to test the waters and cull collective intelligence, creativity, and knowledge through crowdsourcing efforts like the USAID's launch. The next step in engaging the crowd and leveraging resources is to pilot crowdfunding through one of the government's innovation funds. The idea is simple, partner with a crowdfunding platform to leverage government investments, engaging the community, donors, and subject matter experts to make government funds more catalytic. For those seeking funding, making it through a government-vetted competition lends credibility to projects that need an additional round of funding from other investors. While there is no shortage of viable projects that seek support from government innovation funds, there is a shortage of capital. Crowdfunding platforms provide a solution, and a market, for those great ideas.

2. Reach beyond the United States

Crowdfunding is not new. Artists, entrepreneurs, students, philanthropists, and caused-based groups have been tapping into their networks and online platforms for years to help finance their efforts. What diplomacy can do is help take this phenomenon global. While crowdfunding originated in the U.S. and is on the rise in the region (over 72 percent of crowdfunding in 2013 is predicted to stem from the U.S.), the real potential is to provide alternative financing to projects and businesses in emerging markets. The World Bank's preliminary estimate of the potential crowdfunding market in developing countries could reach over $95 billion in the next 25 years. If the platforms that have democratized funding in the U.S. can scale globally, we will see more locally driven solutions to regional challenges that take projects and businesses global, potentially loosening up billions of dollars in capital and spurring economic growth.

3. Incubate locally; educate globally

Development agencies, such as MCC and USAID, have identified local ownership of projects as key to their success. If local communities make the best incubators for local solutions, then building local capacity through providing crowdfunding education and training to emerging markets is essential. Government can mobilize partners globally, help support enabling environments for crowdfunding, and provide access to educational resources and training, ensuring they reach those in need of access to alternative finance. Successfully running a crowdfunding campaign means developing new skills to help sustain an initiative—how to market the idea, engage the audience, and tell a compelling story. Crowdfunding can help incubate and support local solutions to local challenges, develop capacity of new partner organizations, and help raise the profile and sustainability of a program, initiative, business, or cause promote.

Next Steps For Crowdfunding Globally

While crowdfunding is on the rise in the U.S., United Kingdom, and Australia, limitations to global growth exist. Two key issues require further attention to responsibly and effectively accelerate growth: protection against fraud and the know-how to implement projects once they have been funded. While crowdfunding fraud cases are low—the public nature of campaigns, combined with the collective intelligence of social media and consumers serve as a check on spurious projects—ensuring proposals are viable should be a priority for any government piloted crowdfunding initiatives. This means partnering with a reputable crowdfunding platform that can work directly with government to help curate proposals (whether cause-based or business-oriented), vet potential recipients, and provide training to project leaders on how to successfully leverage crowdfunding.

The question remains: what ensures a project will be sustainable beyond initial government funding? Addressing this requires providing educational tools and training from experts on how to successfully run and implement a crowdfunded project. A challenge echoed across the globe is that community projects, non-profits, and small businesses lack the expert backing, technical skills, network, and capital to implement funded projects in a sustainable or scalable way. Government support of crowdfunding should include partnerships that invest in training and capacity building of those leading crowdfunding projects. The acceleration of crowdfunding globally needs to be met with donor and investor education, the adoption of due diligence practices that help root out fraud and partnerships that can help transfer skills and best practices to those seeking to develop projects. Is crowdfunding a panacea in the new era of fiscal austerity? No, it is another tool in the arsenal of diplomacy that can help do more with less, engage local communities in solutions and sift out the best ideas on open and global platforms. It may not change the way government does business, but it deserves a try.

Critical Thinking

1. What lies behind a successful crowdfunding source?
2. What role can government play to make crowdfunding a success?
3. How can crowdfunding impact different sectors of the society?

Create Central

www.mhhe.com/createcentral

Internet References

About.com—Crowdfunding
   http://crowdfunding.about.com/od/Research-on-crowdfunding/fl/How-Crowdfunding-Improves-the-Economy.htm

Crowdfunding Deep Impact
   http://crowdfundingdeepimpact.com/

New York Times
   http://www.nytimes.com/2014/02/08/your-money/crowdfundings-effect-on-venerable-nonprofits-raises-concern.html?_r=0

StartUp Beat
   http://startupbeat.com/2013/11/14/crowdfunding-moves-next-level-jobs-acts-title-ii-effects-startup-fundraising-id3564/

Article   Prepared by: Sudip Ghosh, *Penn State University—Berks*

Should China Worry About a GDP Slowdown?

Growth in China seems to be slowing. Will political instability rise?

Matt Schiavenza

Learning Outcomes

After reading this article, you will be able to:

- Understand the importance of China in the world economy.
- Explain reasons for China's slowdown.
- Explain steps taken by the Chinese government to tackle such problems.

For years, the conventional wisdom about China's GDP was this: if the country didn't meet its target of 8 percent annualized growth, political instability would result. The reasoning behind this wisdom is pretty simple: the Chinese Communist Party, having long ago forfeited its ideological legitimacy, depends solely on providing economic growth in order to stay in power. So long as enough people prosper, they'll put up with a fair amount of repression and corruption. But as soon as economic growth slows, China could be in for a rude awakening.

Has the time come? China's GDP grew by only 7.8 percent in 2012, its worst showing in over a decade, and the numbers for the first quarter of 2013 are even worse: just 7.7 percent, below the 8 percent forecasted by a *Wall Street Journal* survey of economists. To make matters worse, there's some question that the actual number is even lower: some economists are questioning the accuracy of China's inflation statistics, which would mean that real growth is lower still.

Should Beijing be worried about political unrest, then? Probably not, at least in the short term.

For one, China's economic slowdown is, in part, a consequence of demographic changes sweeping the country. According to Yiping Huang, a scholar at Beijing University, the downward shift in China's economy neatly mirrors the decline in the country's working-age population—there were 3.5 million fewer people of working age in the country in 2012 than there were in 2011, a far cry from a decade ago when this figure increased annually. As a result, the economy can slow without a corresponding rise in unemployment. And unemployment, more than anything else, is what Beijing fears can trigger political unrest.

Secondly, a GDP slowdown may help Beijing tackle some of the structural problems with the economy, once described by former Premier Wen Jiabao as "unbalanced, uncoordinated, and unsustainable." Patrick Chovanec, an economist who has written extensively about the Chinese economy, says that "if China slowed for the right reasons, by being more selective with their investments, and moving toward more consumption, a slight slowdown would actually be a good thing." In other words, a slowdown can help tackle a number of issues that threaten China's long-term health—income inequality and environmental issues being two of the bigger ones—as well as mitigate the country's looming bad debt program.

If anything, a bigger risk to political stability in China is an economic collapse rather than a gradual slowdown. A cataclysmic financial crisis—precipitated, perhaps, by the popping of one of China's housing bubbles—that resulted in the depletion of investor savings could unleash far more public anger than a slight drop in GDP growth. And even then, Beijing has taken steps in the last three years to cool its housing bubbles, tightening mortgage lending requirements and placing limits on where Chinese people may buy houses. Though these issues are real concerns, Nicholas Consonery, a China analyst at Eurasia Group, says that the overall risk of an economic meltdown in China remains low.

In the long term, of course, political dissent threatens the Chinese Communist Party—just as it does any authoritarian regime. But for now, the idea that China has to maintain 8 percent growth to survive doesn't apply. "The new benchmark figure," Consonery told me, "ought to be 7.5 percent."

Critical Thinking

1. How do you assess China's growth?
2. Try to figure out ways to entice China to abide by international rules and to make their market more accessible to other nations.

Create Central

www.mhhe.com/createcentral

Internet References

www.foreignpolicy.com/articles/2010/01/04/123000000000000

http://articles.economictimes.indiatimes.com/2013-06-26/news/40206672
_1_chief-economist-asia-ex-japan-decent-growth-rob-subbaraman

www.nber.org/digest/nov06/w12249.html

www.businessinsider.com/world-bank-cuts-chinas-growth-forecast-and
-warns-of-a-possible-sharp-slowdown-2013-6

Article   Prepared by: Sudip Ghosh, *Penn State University—Berks*

Interest in Pot Revenue at New High

JOEL CONNELLY

Learning Outcomes

After reading this article, you will be able to:

- See economic benefits regarding marijuana sales.

- Recognize the potential benefits cannabis sales have for state revenues.

"Cash starved legislatures are seeing dollar signs in dime bags—with talk that a tax on marijuana could pump hundreds of millions or even billions into budgets still reeling from the recession," the web site Politico reported on Thursday.

Even the *Washington Times,* a conservative capital paper published by followers of the Rev. Sun Myung Moon, is writing about marijuana's tax potential.

This state's Office of Financial Management, during the 2012 debate over Initiative 502, predicted that regulating and taxing growth, production and sale of cannabis would yield $296 million to the state by FY 2014, and put $565 million into state coffers in FY 2017. Local tax revenues would total $16.26 million in FY 2014, rising to $35.5 million in FY 2017.

The State House of Representatives recently voted to put a big chunk of anticipated marijuana revenue into early learning programs.

Reps. Earl Blumenauer, D-Oregon, and Jared Polis, D-Colorado, sponsors of marijuana reform legislation in Congress, wrote recently:

Assuming increased legal consumption and reduction in prices, a $50 per ounce tax (on marijuana sales) would raise an estimated revenue of $20 billion annually. This represents a unique opportunity to save ruined lives, wasted enforcement and prison costs, while simultaneously creating a new industry, with new jobs and revenues that will improve the federal budget outlook.

Hopes shouldn't get too high. The federal budget deficit this year is about $1 trillion. A Tax Policy Center study has pegged revenue at only about half of what Blumenauer and Polis are talking about.

There is, however, one major saving: The U.S. spent an estimated $5.5 billion on marijuana enforcement last year. In New York City, for instance, police made an estimated 440,000 arrests for low-level marijuana possession in the last decade, consuming more than one million man-hours of police time.

Reps. Blumenauer and Polis are borrowing from the playbooks of Washington and Colorado.

Under Blumenauer's Marijuana Tax Equity Act, a 50 percent excise tax would be slapped on the first sale of marijuana, from the producer to the processor, similar to taxing of alcohol and tobacco. Producers, importers and manufacturers would pay a $1,000 a year occupational tax. The Internal Revenue Service would deliver regular reports recommending improvements in taxation of pot.

Polis is sponsoring the Ending Federal Marijuana Prohibition Act, which would end pot's draconian classification under the Controlled Substances Act. It would transfer regulation of cannabis from the Drug Enforcement Administration to a renamed Bureau of Alcohol, Tobacco, Marijuana, Firearms and Explosives agency.

Initiative 502 imposes a $250 application fee and a $1,000 issuance/renewal fee for each marijuana licensee through the Washington State Liquor Control Board. The initiative creates marijuana excise taxes equal to 25 percent of the selling price on each wholesale sale and retail sale of marijuana from a licensed producer, processor or retailer.

The Colorado legalization measure provided for an excise tax of no more than 15 percent: A state tax force recently recommended a combined excise tax/sales tax of up to 25 percent.

While recreational use of marijuana is now legal under Washington law, it is probably more open and widespread in California than any other state, and supports the economies of the Golden State's north coast counties.

The state chapter of the National Organization for Reform of Marijuana laws has estimated that a $50 per ounce sales tax on marijuana sales in California would yield $1.2 billion.

Critical Thinking

1. Explain the link between legalizing marijuana and its revenue potential for cash-strapped states.
2. Explain how opponents can see it as a potential for heavy abuse for the users.
3. What is the widely held view of the societal cost of marijuana legalization?

Create Central

www.mhhe.com/createcentral

Internet References

https://mmjbusinessdaily.com/2013/03/21/us-medical-marijuana-sales-estimated-at-1-5b-in-2013-cannabis-industry-could-quadruple-by-2018

www.businessweek.com/debateroom/archives/2010/03/legalize_mariju.html

www.forbes.com/fdc/welcome_mjx.shtml

http://multistate.com/insider/?p=557

Article   Prepared by: Sudip Ghosh, *Penn State University—Berks*

Bitcoin: why Businesses are Buying in, Despite Critics and Start-Up Woes

GLORIA GOODALE

Learning Outcomes

After reading this article, you will be able to:

- Better understand bitcoins.
- Understand bitcoin payment mechanics.
- Discuss international interest in bitcoins.

Despite its well-publicized troubles, including volatile and plunging currency values, the trendy new form of payment known as Bitcoin has a growing allure for many businesses, both online and in the real world.

The cool factor as well as the cash factor—the absence of transaction fees—are the main reasons for a move into what the casual observer might consider a risky form of money. Two recent Bitcoin exchange failures and the death of a Bitcoin CEO have thrown a pall over Bitcoin in the minds of many.

In particular, new businesses whose profit margins are often razor-thin in their debut years are thrilled at having an option to avoid the 3 percent fees they must pay to credit card companies, on average. And if they can be seen riding the hottest new pop culture wave while they do it, so much the better.

"We are trying to be innovators," says David Daneshgar, cofounder of the Los Angeles-based BloomNation, a new online floral business that connects buyers directly with the local florists who will deliver the arrangements.

"We want to be progressive and change the way people buy flowers, and using Bitcoin is part of that change," he adds.

Tapping into the Bitcoin community has had some surprise benefits, Mr. Daneshgar says. "If you follow the discussion threads on the online Bitcoin forums, you see how supportive they are of businesses that accept Bitcoin," he says.

He and his partner saw that almost immediately after adopting Bitcoin into their payment options, visitors to their website who actually bought flowers nearly doubled. Bitcoin shoppers "come to the site already prepared to buy because they want to support us," he says, in contrast with many who are just comparison shopping. "It's a perfect fit for us," he says, adding with a laugh, "Who knew Bitcoin users were such romantics?"

The commercial embrace of this new payment option is documented in a January report from PricewaterhouseCoopers entitled, "Digital Disruptor, How Bitcoin Is Driving Innovation in Entertainment, Media, and Communications."

The survey of 1,000 online shoppers found a 42 percent consumer awareness of the new method. Further, according to the report, consumers are "highly interested in using Bitcoins to download/stream TV shows, movies, or music (38 percent) and purchase TV shows, movies, or sporting event tickets (39 percent), as well as Internet services (39 percent)."

It's not just small businesses entering the fray. The retail website Overstock.com recently began accepting the digital currency and is currently taking in about $30,000 per day using Bitcoin— about 1 percent of its roughly $3.6 million daily sales, according to TechCrunch. TechCrunch, which is devoted to analyzing start-up technology, estimates that Overstock will push that number to six figures by the 2014 holidays.

In addition, some A-level venture capitalists are funding a number of companies that will raise the level of the game, says Campbell Harvey, a professor of international finance at Duke University in Durham, N.C., who teaches a course in cryptocurrency. Netscape founder and now tech venture capitalist Marc Andreessen, for instance, helped launch Coinbase this past year, with a $25 million round of funding from his VC firm, Andreessen Horowitz, infusing the Bitcoin marketplace with larger resources for developing security protocols, among other goals.

Bitcoin is still a young technology, Professor Harvey says in an e-mail, adding that it has the potential "to be massively disruptive" to the world of payments. As with any young technology, he adds, "there will be some growing pains."

An unregulated currency also appeals to those who say there is too much government involvement in private business, says New Orleans entrepreneur David Crais, co-founder of the New Orleans chapter of Health 2.0, a consortium that helps medical professionals run their businesses.

Across the Deep South, where the tea party has strong roots, there is a growing acceptance of Bitcoin "as a way to get the Federal Reserve out of banking," he says.

Many of the doctors he advises across the region who have had a growing number of uninsured cash patients are turning to Bitcoin. It's not so much a desire to do anything that is a benefit to their own business, he says; rather, "it's really about being supportive of what Bitcoin can do for their libertarian ideas."

Of course, fundamental to any enthusiasm from businesses is their ability to convert the highly volatile Bitcoin almost immediately into traditional cash. In the case of BloomNation, that would mean dollars. "We don't store the Bitcoin," Daneshgar says. BloomNation uses the exchange company BitPay to make the currency conversion, virtually instantaneously.

San Diego firm Robo3DPrinter has been accepting Bitcoin for some three months, though so far has made very few sales with the currency.

"We accept bitcoins because it is on the cutting edge right now in technology," says CEO Braydon Moreno. The fact that it is an intangible virtual currency being accepted by the public as a way to barter and trade goods "without sustaining hefty fees on either side is just very fresh and exciting to us," he adds.

It is old school in its ideals and simplicity, Mr. Moreno says, "but new school in its sophistication," using technology for trading.

For the time being, Moreno says, his firm does not convert Bitcoin immediately to dollars, preferring to store them in online wallets.

The recent failure of MtGox, the largest Bitcoin exchange, did worry him.

"If we moved into a much higher volume of sales, we'd probably be exchanging the Bitcoin every day just to make sure we don't lose value," he says.

Businesses are finding a Bitcoin "community" that values the trendy new form of payment, while avoiding the risks of an unregulated currency by converting bitcoins, sometimes quickly, to cash.

Critical Thinking

1. What are bitcoins?
2. Why are businesses interested in bitcoins as modes of payment?
3. How are bitcoins different from mainstream currencies?

Create Central

www.mhhe.com/createcentral

Internet References

Investopedia
   http://www.investopedia.com/articles/investing/052014/why-bitcoins-value-so-volatile.asp

The Verge
   http://www.theverge.com/2014/2/26/5449218/bitcoins-too-big-to-fail-moment

Economic Policy Journal
   http://www.economicpolicyjournal.com/2014/03/cnn-new-irs-rules-make-using-bitcoins.html

The Economist
   http://www.economist.com/blogs/freeexchange/2014/04/money

Article   Prepared by: Sudip Ghosh, *Penn State University—Berks*

Is 'Amnesty' a Possibility Now?

Immigration reform may pass Congress in 2013.

DAVID GRANT

Learning Outcomes

After reading this article, you will be able to:

- Understand the challenges facing amnesty policies.

- Ascertain the economic impacts of granting amnesty.

- Explain the reasons why amnesty is considered to be such a charged topic.

The momentum of President Obama's resounding victory in November's election—with a big push from Latinos and other minority groups—has catapulted immigration policy to the top of Washington's 2013 agenda, making reform not only possible but also likely.

The shift in the political conversation has been so dramatic that even a pathway to citizenship for some of the estimated 12 million undocumented immigrants in the United States—long rejected out of hand by most Republicans and some Democrats—could be part of the deal.

The task is momentous. It involves weighing the wishes of industries from agriculture to high-tech, as well as the sensitivities of opening the door to immigrant workers at a time when unemployment remains high.

The past only reinforces the potential difficulties ahead. In 1986, Republicans felt betrayed when Democrats stripped the enforcement provisions from a bill that offered citizenship to some 3 million illegal immigrants. By 2005, the issue had become so politically toxic to conservatives that they blocked President George W. Bush's push for a new round of immigration reform.

Yet with Election 2012 highlighting the electoral consequences of America's changing demographics, the next year appears to be ripe for compromise. How reforms might take shape could be a major point of contention between the parties, but lawmakers on both sides suddenly see an opportunity for what could be their most expansive achievement of 2013.

"It has to be in 2013," says Rep. Raúl Labrador (R) of Idaho, an immigration lawyer who thundered into Congress in the tea party wave of 2010. "If we wait until 2014, it's going to be election time. And you know how efficient we are here during election time."

Recent weeks have seen a flurry of activity on Capitol Hill. In the Senate, a "Gang of Eight"—led by longtime immigration reformers Sen. Chuck Schumer (D) of New York and Republican Sens. John McCain of Arizona and Lindsey Graham of South Carolina—has added freshman Sens. Michael Bennett (D) of Colorado and Mike Lee (R) of Utah, while potential 2010 presidential aspirant Sen. Marco Rubio (R) of Florida leads his own initiative.

Members of the House have seen movement too. "One thing clearly has changed," says Rep. Luis Gutierrez (D) of Illinois, the lawmaker who co-wrote a 2005 comprehensive immigration reform measure with now Sen.-elect Jeff Flake (R) of Arizona. "Nobody is talking about self-deportation. Nobody is talking about how [Arizona's controversial immigration law] should be the standard applied across the land. Nobody is talking about vetoing the DREAM Act," which offers a path to citizenship for some young undocumented immigrants.

"We are having wonderful conversations," Representative Gutierrez says.

That more moderate tone from the GOP is what the November election has wrought.

In a postelection analysis and poll of Latino voters, Republican polling group Resurgent Republic offered a searing critique of the GOP's political strategy of pumping up turnout among white voters, often by championing hard-line policies on immigration issues that turn off key Asian and Hispanic voters.

"Republicans have run out of persuadable white voters," wrote conservative pollster Whit Ayres and Jennifer Korn, the head of the right-leaning Hispanic Leadership Network, in a recent research memo. "Trying to win a national election by gaining a larger and larger share of a smaller and smaller portion of the electorate is a losing political proposition."

Between 2008 and 2012, white voters shrank two percentage points to 72 percent of the electorate, while Asian and Latino voters expanded a percentage point each to 3 percent and 10 percent, respectively.

While GOP presidential candidate Mitt Romney won 60 percent of white voters, 71 percent of Latinos and 73 percent of Asian-Americans backed Mr. Obama—up four percentage points and 11 percentage points from 2008, respectively.

And those numbers of minority voters are only going to grow. For the next two decades, 50,000 Latino voters will turn 18 every month, adding an additional New Hampshire of voters to the US each year into the 2030s.

While Resurgent Republic's poll showed that Hispanics aren't singularly focused on immigration issues, Republican politicians who favor immigration reform see the issue as primary: The GOP's message of conservative family values, entrepreneurship, and individual freedom won't reach Latino voters unless the immigration question is solved.

"This is like a wall that stops the other issues from getting through," says Rep. Mario Diaz-Balart (R) of Florida, a long-time immigration reform advocate. "And while that wall is there, the Republican Party has a serious problem."

House Speaker John Boehner (R) of Ohio signaled a shift when he told ABC News a day after the election that "a comprehensive approach [to immigration] is long overdue, and I'm confident that the president, myself, others, can find the common ground to take care of this issue once and for all."

That's a departure from previous immigration-reform attempts, in which the GOP brass wasn't on board.

Perhaps just as important, though, is that several leading lawmakers with near-pristine conservative credentials are also involved.

Two tea party superstars—Senators Rubio and Lee, both of whom knocked out establishment Republican figures to win their seats—are going to be key players in any reform.

In the House, the involvement of House Judiciary chairman Rep. Bob Goodlatte (R) of Virginia and Representative Labrador of Idaho can provide cover to conservative lawmakers from the party's right flank.

"The fact that you're going to have strong conservative voices helping lead this debate is going to be critical to solving it instead of using it as a political wedge," says Rep. Steve Scalise (R) of Louisiana, the incoming chairman of the Republican Study Committee, the largest and most conservative caucus in the House.

It's notable that both Labrador and Rubio believe, in one way or another, in a path to citizenship for some illegal immigrants, even while they leave open just who can get on that path.

Some conservatives say that any form of citizenship given to illegal immigrants—no matter the conditions attached to it—constitutes an "amnesty," which is a guarantee only of more illegal immigration unless the nation's borders are firmly secured and stringent workplace verification systems are put in place.

But a recent poll by George Washington University and Politico found 62 percent of Americans support a proposal that would allow illegal immigrants to earn citizenship over a period of several years, with 40 percent strongly supporting such a measure. Only 35 percent opposed it.

Some Democrats on the Hill are extending a friendly hand to the GOP. When the Congressional Hispanic Caucus—which is entirely Democratic—offered its vision for immigration reform, for example, it served up principles rather than a specific bill, a

move received by Republicans as attempting to maximize common ground.

But Democrats also know they are in a position of power.

"I think you've got a realization on the part of GOP leadership not just in the House but in the Republican Party writ large that if they don't do something about it, they aren't going to win the presidency again," says Rep. Zoe Lofgren (D) of California, a leading immigration reform advocate.

For that reason, she says, Republicans "aren't going to get the credit" for pushing immigration through, but they "can still get the blame if they block" it.

Latino advocacy groups and labor unions, emboldened by the community's growing electoral power, vow to take the fight to those who stand in immigration reform's way in 2013.

"This comprehensive immigration reform for the Latino community is personal. The fact that we've come out in record numbers in 2012 was personal. And that's a calculation that members of Congress don't understand," says Maria Teresa Kumar, executive director of Voto Latino. "If they are not with us, 2014 may not look pretty with them."

The president, too, has political pressure to pursue immigration reform. He has already come up short once on immigration-reform promises: In 2009, he said that a comprehensive immigration solution would be a top priority.

Yet his first term also saw record numbers of undocumented immigrants deported. Only this summer, after he directed immigration officials to defer deportation of some young illegal immigrants, was he seen as making good on promises to the Latino community.

"The president says that his biggest failure in the first term was not moving forward with immigration reform," says Hector Sanchez, executive director of the Labor Council for Latin American Advancement. "The Latino community decided to give him a second chance."

Obama has publicly vowed to make immigration reform an immediate priority in his second term, which could begin just on the other side of the "fiscal cliff" negotiations.

"He's the one who has the mandate on this subject; he's the guy who got the voters who care most intensely about this," says Bruce Morrison, a former Democratic congressman from Connecticut who was involved in immigration reform efforts in the 1980s and early '90s.

But even while the parties broadly agree on the need to pursue immigration reform, how to do it remains up in the air.

Both Rubio and Labrador—like many Republicans—favor breaking up the immigration issue into smaller pieces.

Rubio argues that before Congress deals with the millions of undocumented immigrants, it must prove to the American people that it can secure US borders and establish an effective workplace-verification system. Labrador says that he prefers a handful of bills moving simultaneously, with different coalitions able to support each measure.

Obama and Democrats in Congress favor a single comprehensive immigration bill, believing that taking one difficult but all-encompassing vote is more secure for lawmakers than having to vote for a half-dozen or more specific proposals.

"It's not a policy decision. It's a strategy decision, but it's an important one," says Representative Lofgren.

While Democrats and Republicans have been negotiating immigration reform for years, lawmakers also say it is vital that small groups of negotiators not hand down a fully formed bill to either chamber with an effective "take it or leave it" sticker on top.

"I think it's important that we listen to our colleagues; it's important that we listen to the American people," says Representative Diaz-Balart. "I think it would be a grave mistake if we try to ram something down and pretend like we have all the answers."

And while Republicans are on board now, there's a reason they've been hesitant to tackle immigration reform in the past. For one, a vocal part of their base views any form of citizenship for illegal immigrants as a repudiation of the rule of law. Whether these voters—or their representatives—can be persuaded to accept amnesty is an open question.

'There are a multitude of reasons [that politicians now support reform].'

—REP. LUIS GUTIERREZ (D)

"We can negotiate about the DREAMers and things like that, but the vast, vast majority of the people who are here illegally—say 12 million people—I think they came here after the age of 18. They knowingly violated the law, and we have to have respect for our law," Labrador says.

Moreover, increasing legal immigration above the current level of 1 million annually could be seen as a blow to those born in America.

Hurting "the American worker with bad immigration policy is not going to get [Republicans] more Hispanic votes," says Roy Beck, executive director of Numbers USA, a group that advocates lower immigration levels. "They've got to do something else."

In that respect, increasing legal immigration might be a difficult sell in 2013.

"I do not see Congress acting in this area in a robust way until the labor market is stronger," says Andrew Schoenholtz, deputy director for the Institute for the Study of International Migration at Georgetown University. "Just how strong is hard to tell."

And then there are the questions that perhaps matter most in the Beltway: Whose plan is on the table first? Which party sets the initial terms for debate?

"The best thing to happen is for some bipartisan thing to get out there first. What's wrong with the debate is winners and losers," Mr. Morrison says. "If you think you're going to beat the other guy into submission with your plan, regardless of what side you're on, the reaction you're going to get is opposition."

A political environment more favorable to immigration reform, however, builds upon longstanding bipartisan relationships. Gutierrez and Rep. Paul Ryan (R) of Wisconsin, back from the campaign trail as Mr. Romney's vice presidential running mate, smiled broadly as they walked together into the House chamber for a vote in mid-December.

Gutierrez, a progressive Hispanic Democrat from Chicago, and Representative Ryan, a man Democrats caricatured as pushing Grandma off a cliff with his proposals to change entitlement programs for the elderly, may seem like an odd couple.

But back in 2005, Ryan was an original co-sponsor of Gutierrez's immigration-reform proposal.

"They've been good friends," says a Ryan spokesman. "They've had a working relationship on this issue and really do see it in the same, pragmatic way."

In Ryan, Gutierrez sees a model for a conservative coming to the issue out of conviction, not political expediency.

"I think he's doing it because it's a reflection of his deep Catholic values, and he wants to get it done," Gutierrez says. "There are a multitude of reasons that people have [come to support immigration reform, and] for the most part what I've seen is they are very sincere and they are genuine."

"All we're doing," Gutierrez says, "is catching up."

Critical Thinking

1. How can we meet the challenges that amnesty presents?
2. If amnesty is granted to undocumented workers in the United States, how will it affect employment?

Create Central

www.mhhe.com/createcentral

Internet References

http://articles.latimes.com/keyword/amnestyoptions
www.time.com/time/magazine/article/0,9171,1630543,00.html
www.policymic.com/articles/24236/immigration-reform-2013-why
-is-amnesty-such-a-dirty-word
www.weeklystandard.com/articles/amnesty-next-time_722057.html

Article   Prepared by: Sudip Ghosh, *Penn State University—Berks*

New Study Suggests eBooks Could Negatively Affect How We Comprehend What We Read

MEMET WALKER

Learning Outcomes

After reading this article, you will be able to:

- Understand the cost benefits of an ebook.

- Understand the results of the ebook study.

For many students, ebooks are a great and inexpensive tool.

But do they negatively affect how we comprehend what we read? A new study might drain the proverbial juice in their Kindle's batteries.

Earlier this month, Heather Schugar, an associate education professor of education at West Chester University, and her husband, Jordan Schugar, an instructor there, presented their findings which showed a small sample of middle school students given ebooks retained less information about what they read compared to students given the same information in print.

"(The students with ebooks) were much more motivated to read," she says, "but they were also able to re-tell less. Their ability to answer questions wasn't quite as strong when they were reading interactive ebooks."

In a nutshell, the problems with many ebooks, the Schugars say, are all of the flashy gimmicks, fun interactive designs and ability to wander from the text that distract readers from the task of actually, well. . . reading.

"It's like PowerPoint," he says, "At first, everyone wanted their slides to fly in and dissolve and have all of those effects. And all of that became very distracting from the message."

Meredith Broussard, an assistant journalism professor at Temple University, says she's banned ebooks from her classrooms for years.

"I like technology, I embrace technology," Broussard says. "But I'm a little old fashioned. I like having a book next to me."

Part of the issue, she says, was something so simple as students not even being able to open up to the same page in class.

"It takes class time," Broussard says. "People can't work their interface, or their battery's dead, or they can't find a plug."

Broussard says, for her, it's all about design, and the printed book is a better interface for what she does in her classroom.

"I teach small seminars where it depends on face-to-face interaction," she says, "and when we can all open up to the same page, it helps."

Gloria Mark, a professor of informatics at University of California, Irvine, has studied the gamut of technology.

Mark says she also sees how ebooks can not only be difficult for some students and instructors, but also distracting for them.

"If you reach a point in the book that's boring, and you know you can check Facebook or email or search something on the web," Mark says, "people can switch very rapidly."

If an eBook is self-contained, she says, this kind of behavior may be less likely.

"But then maybe they'll switch between different books on their device," Mark says.

For Jonathan Patten, 22, a junior digital arts major at La Salle University, ebooks are a cheaper alternative to lugging big books around.

Many of his textbooks, he says, cost over 100 dollars, where the eBook version can sometimes be found for 10 to 15.

"It's a godsend," Patten says.

He admits they can make it easier to become distracted, but also says one of their benefits is how easy it is to quickly search through the text.

"You don't have to *sift through* pages and pages of material," Patten says.

Rahi Talukder, 22, a graduate student studying bioengineering at University of Denver, says she definitely prefers print.

"I've tried studying from ebooks online," Talukder says, "but I physically need the book in my hand."

"You have to physically zoom in and out. It's a pain."

Still, Schugar says it's important to understand ebooks aren't all bad.

"We're not saying ebooks are bad by any means," she says. "We just need to really think about how reading may be different where we're reading from a tablet environment."

Critical Thinking

1. Weigh the cost benefits of using an ebook against the results of the study.

2. Do you feel that the results of the ebook study reflect how you would comprehend and retain information using an ebook instead of a traditional book? Explain.

Create Central

www.mhhe.com/createcentral

Internet References

Education Week
http://blogs.edweek.org/edweek/DigitalEducation/2014/04/early_concerns_about_e-books_e_1.html

Forbes
http://www.forbes.com/sites/janetnovack/2012/05/18/should-college-students-be-forced-to-buy-e-books/

Investopedia
http://www.investopedia.com/financial-edge/0812/e-books-vs.-print-books.aspx

SEEN—Southeast Education Network
http://seenmagazine.us/articles/article-detail/articleid/3525/the-future-of-ebooks-in-the-classroom.aspx

Unit 6

ADDITIONAL ARTICLES

Article

Broke in the Burbs

AMY KELLER

Lakeland is known for high school football, its quaint downtown and a unique collection of Frank Lloyd Wright architecture at Florida Southern College. Its central location, meanwhile, has helped to transform the Polk County suburbs into a popular bedroom community for Tampa and Orlando commuters, who moved there in droves over the past two decades.

These days, Lakeland also claims a more dubious distinction. According to a report published in January by the Brookings Institution, Lakeland had the fifth-highest suburban poverty rate in the nation in 2008. According to the study, 75,075 people in Lakeland's surrounding suburbs—15.8% of the population—live below the poverty level of $21,834 for a family of four. Within Lakeland's city limits, meanwhile, 12,182 people, or 13.3% of the population, live in poverty.

The explosion of poverty in Lakeland's suburbs mirrors a national trend—between 2000 and 2008, according to the Brookings' study, the country's largest metro areas saw the poor population in their suburbs grow by 25%—a rate about five times faster than in cities.

Brookings attributes the shifting "geography of poverty" to the fact that current economic downturn has taken a "toll on traditionally more suburbanized industries," and that more job loss has been concentrated in the suburbs as well.

Suburban pockets of Miami, Tampa and Palm Bay have also been hard hit. Nearly 70% of Tampa Bay's 337,470 poor live in the suburbs, the study shows. Brookings concludes that this "ongoing shift in the geography of American poverty" will require "regional scale collaboration by policymakers and social service providers in order to effectively address the needs of a poor population that is increasingly suburban."

Changes in Poverty 2000–08		
Tampa-St. Petersburg-Clearwater		
	No. of Poor	Poverty Rate/Chg. Since 2000
Cities	102,579	15.3%/–0.1%
Suburbs	234,891	11.7%/2.1%
Orlando		
	No. of Poor	Poverty Rate/Chg. Since 2000
Cities	43,732	18.9%/3%
Suburbs	197,004	11.0%/1%
Palm Bay		
	No. of Poor	Poverty Rate/Chg. Since 2000
Cities	10,087	10%/0.5%
Suburbs	44,729	10.5%/1%

Top 10 Poverty Rates in the Suburbs 2008	
1. McAllen, Texas	36.7%
2. El Paso, Texas	31.0
3. Bakersfield, Calif.	24.2
4. Fresno, Calif.	18.8
5. Lakeland	**15.8**
6. Modesto, Calif.	14.6
7. Little Rock, Ark.	14.2
8. Jackson, Miss.	14.0
9. Augusta-Richmond Co., Ga.-S.C.	14.0
10. Albuquerque, N.M.	13.6

Change in Projected Poverty Rates	
Select Florida Metro Areas (2008–09)	
Metro Area	**Percentage Point Change**
Cape Coral-Fort Myers	3.8
Lakeland-Winter Haven	3.3
Orlando-Kissimmee	3.2
Tampa-St. Petersburg-Clearwater	3.2
Palm Bay-Melbourne-Titusville	3.0
Jacksonville	2.9
Miami-Fort Lauderdale-Pompano Beach	2.5

Article

CRE: The Cracked Glass Slipper?

CRE exposure and delinquencies are on the rise for Ninth District banks, but the full fallout is difficult to gauge.

RONALD A. WIRTZ

It's a common assumption that commercial real estate represents the proverbial "other shoe" for the banking industry, and that CRE portfolios are poised to reclobber banks after many had only begun to recover from a deep recession and meltdown in housing markets.

For a number of reasons, it's hard to say how closely the health of the banking sector is tied to the commercial real estate market. Without doubt, the banking sector will experience—and is already seeing—fallout from the CRE slump. A notable number of banks have portfolios that exceed regulator guidelines for CRE concentration, particularly for construction and land development loans. In tandem with that trend, delinquency rates for all types of CRE loans are rising.

But it's difficult to gauge or predict bank health based on the current and expected performance of the broader CRE market. For starters, the CRE boom was financed by a number of different sources. The banking industry (including savings institutions) is the single largest holder of outstanding commercial mortgage debt, with about $1.4 trillion of the $2.5 trillion owed nationwide, according to December flow of funds data from the Federal Reserve Board.

A little less than one-quarter of outstanding debt is held in so-called commercial mortgage-backed securities (though virtually no new CMBS debt has been generated since 2007). Life insurance firms have about 10 percent of commercial mortgage debt, and the remaining amount is held by a hodgepodge of sources, including the federal government, real estate investment trusts, finance companies and pension funds.

Unfortunately, no similar estimates exist for CRE financing in the Ninth District, so it's difficult to say how large the CRE pickle jar is for district banks or what submarkets are most exposed. That's not a small matter, given the fact that the annual value of retail CRE transactions in the Twin Cities rose almost 20-fold just from 2001 to 2006, to more than $3 billion, while office CRE transactions rose eightfold during the same period, to $2 billion, according to data from Real Capital Analytics.

Sibling Rivalry?

Within a range of other banking metrics, the scope and nature of the CRE problem is both better and worse than its residential housing predecessor. The district's large banks—those with more than $10 billion in assets—have comparatively low CRE exposure, according to third-quarter Call Report data from the Federal Deposit Insurance Corporation.

But potential problems from CRE are much more widespread among smaller community and regional banks that predominate in the Ninth District. For example, total outstanding CRE debt held by banks with less than $10 billion in assets has more than doubled in real terms since 2000, to $33 billion. Residential loans (traditional mortgages and home equity loans) among this group have also risen, but more slowly, and total about $18 billion (see Chart 1).

Exposure at some banks has crossed certain thresholds that regulators consider prudent; about one in seven banks in the Ninth District have loan concentrations in this sector that exceed bank regulator guidelines.

For example, regulators (including the Federal Reserve) deem a bank's portfolio concentrated if it includes CRE loans in excess of 300 percent of the bank's total risk-based capital. Such concentration can be potentially dangerous because the lack of loan diversification puts a bank in harm's way should an economic shock hit the sector. A total of 39 banks in the district exceeded this 300 percent threshold at the end of September, with

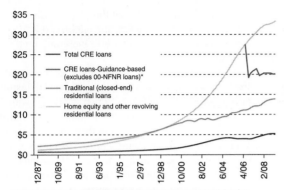

*2006 regulator guidance on CRE loan concentration excludes loans for owner-occupied, nonfarm nonresidential real estate, which is why that segment is split off separately starting in the first quarter of 2007.

Chart 1   District CRE loans growing faster than housing   Merger-adjusted, billions of 2009 dollars Bank with less than $10 billion in assets

Source: Reports of Condition and Income (Call Reports), FDIC

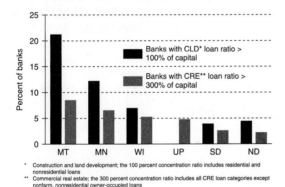

*   Construction and land development; the 100 percent concentration ratio includes residential and nonresidential loans
** Commercial real estate; the 300 percent concentration ratio includes all CRE loan categories except nonfarm, nonresidential owner-occupied loans

Chart 2   CRE and CLD concentration highest in Montana and Minnesota   CRE loan ratios compared with 2006 regulator guidance

Source: Reports of Condition and Income (Call Reports), FDIC

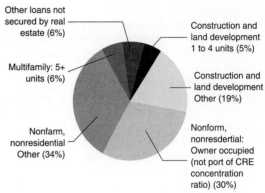

Chart 3   Outstanding loans by CRE sector   Ninth District banks, as of Sept, 30, 2009

Source: Reports of Condition and Income (Call Reports), FDIC

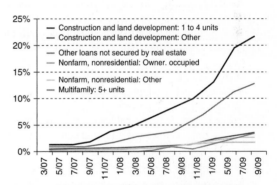

Chart 4   District bank CRE delinquency rates rising

Source: Reports of Condition and Income (Call Reports), FDIC

the highest percentage in Montana and Minnesota (see Chart 2). Exceeding this threshold does not imply imminent demise for a bank. But it is an indicator of enhanced risk, evident by the fact that regulators require more sophisticated and enhanced management practices from these banks.

This CRE loan concentration also is more prevalent among smaller banks. Whereas the housing debacle slammed the nation's largest banks—with assets in the hundreds of billions—no district bank that exceeded the 300 percent ratio had assets exceeding $1 billion in assets, and the large majority were much smaller than even this level.

These concentration figures also do not include so-called owner-occupied nonfarm-nonresidential property—in essence, commercial mortgages to firms that own their office or manufacturing plant, rather than leasing space from a property owner. The rationale for this exclusion is that repayment for such loans does not depend on the swings in supply and demand for commercial buildings themselves; rather, repayment depends on the performance of the company and the broader economy.

This bit of methodological minutia offers both good and bad news. First, this owner-occupied segment of commercial mortgages is big, making up 30 percent of the outstanding CRE debt held by district banks (see Chart 3). That means a large share of CRE lending is, technically speaking, of less concern to regulators in terms of concentrated risk in this sector.

At the same time, loan performance among owner-occupied borrowers nonetheless has some influence on supply and demand in the broader CRE market and has been worsening; the delinquency rate for owner-occupied commercial loans is currently higher than for nonowner-occupied property loans and is on a steeper trajectory (see Chart 4).

Another indicator of heightened risk is concentrated lending in construction and land development (CLD).

Regulators become concerned when such loans amount to 100 percent or more of a bank's total risk-based capital. The lower guidance ratio for this measure is due to the fact that these loans usually don't generate income until completed, so they can be particularly risky if real estate markets sour. And even more district banks—86, in all—had crossed this guidance threshold as of the end of September, with Montana and Minnesota banks again seeing the largest share. Also notable is the fact that delinquency rates for CLD loans have risen much faster compared with other CRE loans.

Combined, 101 of the 713 commercial banks in the district exceeded at least one of these guidelines; a total of 13 banks violated both guidance measures, with almost half (six) of them in Montana.

With rising delinquency rates as well as a looming threat of maturity default for some loans (discussed in the cover article), lenders and borrowers alike received some helpful guidance from regulators last fall. First, the IRS approved a rule change that allows CRE borrowers to begin negotiating loan modifications before the loans themselves go bad. Previously, such modifications carried tax penalties, typically delaying such negotiations until default was imminent.

Then in late October, bank regulatory agencies (including the Federal Reserve) jointly announced guidelines to help banks "prudently" renew and restructure troubled CRE loans without intensifying the underlying risk to bank capital. The hope is that this change will better align the desire of both regulators and bankers to lift the banking sector to safer ground while loosening credit to the CRE market.

In a joint statement, regulators said new guidelines for loan workouts "recognize that financial institutions face significant challenges when working with commercial real estate borrowers. . . . While CRE borrowers may experience deterioration in their financial condition, many continue to be credit-worthy customers who have the willingness and capacity to repay then debts. In such cases, financial institutions and borrowers may find it mutually beneficial to work constructively together."

While CRE borrowers may experience deterioration in their financial condition, many continue to be creditworthy customers who have the willingness and capacity to repay their debts. In such cases, financial institutions and borrowers may find it mutually beneficial to work constructively together.

Associate Economist Daniel Rozycki and Economist Mark Lueck contributed data and analysis in this article.

Article

Is the Recent Productivity Boom Over?

Daniel J. Wilson

Productivity growth has been quite strong over the past 2½ years, despite a drop in the second quarter of 2010. Many analysts believe that productivity growth must slow sharply in order for the labor market to recover robustly. However, looking at the observable factors underlying recent productivity growth and the patterns of productivity over past recessions and recoveries, a sharp slowdown appears unlikely.

Labor productivity, defined as output per hour of labor, unexpectedly stalled in the second quarter of 2010, falling by a 1.1% annual rate in the total business sector based on data available through the end of August. This follows 2½ years of generally strong productivity growth, which started when the recession began at the end of 2007. In fact, the annualized 2.5% pace of labor productivity growth during the latest recession, which appears to have ended in mid-2009, was the fourth strongest of the 11 recessions since World War II. Post-recession, from the third quarter of 2009 to the second quarter of 2010, productivity grew at an even faster annual pace of 2.8%, even with the second-quarter drop. This strong growth is one reason for the scant downward movement in the unemployment rate despite moderate GDP gains. Businesses have been able to meet demand for their products and services without hiring new workers or increasing the hours of current staff because they are managing to get more from each hour of labor.

Recent rapid gains in productivity beg the questions of where the growth is coming from and whether it is sustainable. They also raise the question of whether the second-quarter drop was just a temporary blip in an otherwise strong productivity trend or the start of a significant productivity slowdown. The strength of the labor market recovery hinges on the answers to these questions. Many forecasters have predicted moderate GDP growth and a reasonably strong recovery in employment over the next year or two. Such a scenario would require a sharp slowdown in productivity growth to about 1% or less.

CSIP Notes appear on an occasional basis. They are prepared under the auspices of the Center for the Study of Income and Productivity.

This Economic Letter examines the risks to this forecast, first looking at how productivity growth has fared in past recessions and recoveries. Then it considers where recent gains have come from. For example, do they reflect more physical capital relative to labor hours, increases in labor quality, or efficiency gains? The findings suggest that productivity growth for the next year or so might very well exceed forecaster expectations, which would put a damper on employment gains.

Productivity Growth in Past Recessions and Recoveries

Productivity growth was strong in the latest recession compared with that registered in past recessions. Figure 1 shows these comparisons using Bureau of Labor Statistics (BLS) seasonally-adjusted quarterly data on real output per labor hour for the nonfarm business sector. Growth

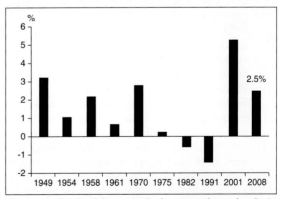

Figure 1 Productivity growth in recessions (peak to trough) Percent change in business output per hour, annual rate

Source: Bureau of Labor Statistics (BLS) and author's calculations.

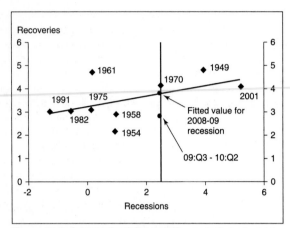

Figure 2   Labor productivity growth, recession vs. recovery Growth from peak to trough (x-axis) vs. growth over 8 quarters since trough (y-axis), annual rate
Source: BLS and author's calculations.

rates are annualized to facilitate comparisons among recessions of different durations. The National Bureau of Economic Research Business Cycle Dating Committee, the standard source for recession dates, has determined that the previous expansion peaked, and the recession began, in December 2007. The committee has not yet determined when, or even if, the latest recession ended. Many analysts believe the business cycle trough occurred sometime around the middle of 2009. Here I assume the third quarter of 2009 was the last quarter of the recession. Using the second quarter for the analysis yields qualitatively similar conclusions. Including third-quarter data, productivity grew at an annualized 2.5% rate during the latest recession. Adjusting for changes over time in the underlying trend rate of productivity growth, which is generally thought to have slowed around 1973 and accelerated after 1995, does not change this conclusion.

Does strong productivity growth in a recession predict strong productivity growth in the subsequent recovery? Figure 2 is a scatter plot characterizing the relationship between productivity growth in past recessions and productivity growth in the subsequent recoveries. Each point represents a particular recession-recovery episode. All post-World War II episodes are shown except that of the very short 1980 recession, whose recovery overlapped with the 1982 recession. The value of the point on the x-axis indicates annualized productivity growth during the recession. The value of the point on the y-axis gives the productivity growth rate during the subsequent recovery, which is defined as the eight quarters following recession.

There is a clear positive correlation, as indicated by the fact that those points with high x-axis values, indicating fast productivity growth during the recession, tend also to have high y-axis values, indicating fast productivity growth during the subsequent recovery. The positively sloping line running through the data points is what is known in statistics as a regression fit line, showing the relationship between productivity growth in recessions and productivity growth in subsequent recoveries in the post-World War II data. The vertical line at the value of 2.5% on the x-axis shows productivity growth in the recent recession. The historical relationship between productivity growth in recessions and recoveries, traced by the regression fit line, predicts that productivity growth for the current recovery will be about 3.8%. Because of the sharp productivity drop in the second quarter, the 2.8% productivity growth from the third quarter of 2009 through the second quarter of 2010 is somewhat below this predicted level. Still, this recovery rate of productivity growth is above the rate during the recession and is well over the roughly 1% pace that many private forecasters have predicted. Adjusting the data for estimates of underlying trend productivity growth dampens the positive relationship somewhat, but the correlation remains positive.

Of course, one should not make too much of a correlation based on nine data points. All the same, since World War II, only in the recovery following the 2001 downturn was productivity growth slower than it was in the recession itself. And that episode may be an exception that proves the rule. Productivity growth in the recovery following the 2001 recession was a strong annualized 3.9%, far above estimates of the underlying structural productivity trend. Many economists point to this strong growth as a key factor in the so-called "jobless recovery" that took place after the 2001 recession. This bodes poorly for employment in the current recovery. Today's forecasts of a sharp productivity slowdown, necessary for robust employment growth, imply a serious departure from history, in which productivity growth in recoveries has generally exceeded growth in recessions.

Where Are Recent Productivity Gains Coming From?

To better understand why labor productivity growth has been so strong over the past few years, it is useful to break down this growth into measurable components. To assess the sources of productivity gains, economists separate growth in output per hour into observable factors related to capital investment and the average skill

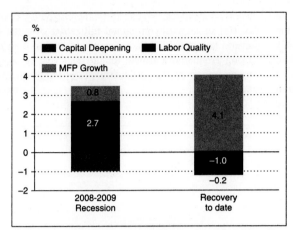

Figure 3   Labor productivity growth decomposition Percent point contributions, annual rate

Source: Author's calculations based on data from Fernald 2009.

level of the workforce. In addition, economists consider unobserved residual factors which are collectively called total- or multi-factor productivity growth (MFP). In other words, a portion of labor productivity growth can be attributed to additions to the quantity of capital in the form of equipment or buildings for each hour of work, a process known as capital deepening. Another portion can be attributed to changes in the "quality" of workers, typically defined as the average education level of the workforce. What's left over—the difference between total measured labor productivity growth and the sum of the contributions from capital deepening and labor quality—are the unmeasured or difficult-to-measure factors that make up multi-factor productivity growth. These may include changes in the intensity of capital and labor utilization, measurement errors in labor hours, and productivity gains due to technological change, improvements in management techniques, greater efficiency of distribution systems, and the like.

Although Bureau of Labor Statistics data on labor productivity are available quarterly, BLS data on capital deepening, labor quality, and multi-factor productivity are only available annually and with a considerable lag. Fernald (2009), however, constructs quarterly data on these factors, which have been updated through the second quarter of 2010 (see http://www.frbsf.org/economics/economists/jfernald/quarterly_tfp.xls).

Using these data, it is possible to analyze labor productivity growth for the recent recession and the recovery through the second quarter of 2010. The results are shown in Figure 3. During the recession, capital deepening was the main factor, contributing 2.7 percentage points to total annualized labor productivity growth. This strong capital

deepening was not because capital investment was particularly robust during the recession. Rather, it reflected a calamitous drop in labor hours combined with weak but positive growth in capital services, a measure of flows coming from physical assets and software.

That is, investment more than kept up with depreciation of existing capital while businesses reduced labor input severely. Labor quality also contributed positively to productivity growth, as businesses disproportionately laid off or didn't hire less-educated workers. Such "up-skilling" is common in recessions. Together, capital deepening and the increase in labor quality accounted for more than 100% of observed labor productivity growth in the recession. The residual multi-factor productivity growth was actually slightly negative.

However, in the recovery, the roles of capital deepening and multi-factor productivity reversed. Growth in employment and hours worked returned to positive territory in late 2009. Capital services, however, were essentially flat during the recovery through the second quarter of 2010. As a result, capital deepening—or shallowing in this case—contributed negatively to productivity. Yet, labor productivity growth accelerated, thanks to 4.1% multi-factor productivity growth.

Where did all this multi-factor productivity growth come from? As noted, the factors behind multi-factor productivity growth—measurement error in hours worked, changes in capital utilization, changes in labor effort, and efficiency gains due to technological or organizational changes—are, by definition, unmeasurable, or at least very difficult to measure, especially in real time. For example, measurement error in hours worked can contribute to measured productivity growth because productivity is typically defined in terms of hours paid, based on data collected quarterly in large-scale BLS surveys. The surveys miss hours actually worked because of such factors as "off-the-books" employment. BLS does report annual survey data on the ratio of hours worked to hours paid, with a substantial lag. The latest year currently is 2008. The magnitude of past year-to-year changes in this ratio suggests that its movements are not likely to explain much of the 4.1% multi-factor productivity growth in the recovery to date. The largest year-over-year change in this ratio from 1976 to 2008 was 0.5%.

Capital utilization, on the other hand, appears to have much more promise as an explanation for the recent multi-factor productivity growth. The Federal Reserve Board's industrial capacity utilization rate, often used as a proxy for capital utilization, has increased 10% since mid-2009. Capital accounts for about one-third of production, with labor accounting for the rest. Hence, capital utilization potentially contributes over 3 percentage points to multi-factor productivity and, by extension, to overall labor productivity growth. Separate data on the capital workweek in the manufacturing sector also suggest a large potential contribution from capital utilization.

Evidence that capital utilization is an important and possibly the primary factor behind the recent strength in productivity growth has important implications for the sustainability of that growth going forward. Although measures of capital utilization have grown rapidly during the recovery to date, they are still well below their historical averages. That suggests there is plenty of room for further increases in capital utilization over the next several quarters. Such increases could lead to continued strong productivity growth for the next year or so, posing an important risk to the strength of the labor market recovery.

DANIEL J. WILSON is a senior economist at the Federal Reserve Bank of San Francisco.

Reprinted with permission from *the FRBSF Economic Letter,* September 2010, by Daniel Wilson. The opinions expressed in this article do not necessarily reflect the views of the management of the Federal Reserve Bank of San Francisco, or of the Board of Governors of the Federal Reserve System.

Article

The Long Term Economic Effects of the BP Oil Spill

JKALAL ASSAR

It is widely acknowledged the BP oil spill will bear severe consequences, and its economic impact might prove to be the most grave.

The BP oil disaster of 2010 has established new financial precedents regarding accidental oil spills, specifically when the ratio of duration to cost is taken into consideration. Relatively enormous sums of money have already been distributed on behalf of the company in response to cleanup costs, stipends paid to displaced workers and businesses, and grants issued to affected state governments. But this pales in comparison to what the total amount will in all probability reach.

The Financial Responsibility of BP Oil

As of 18 June 2010, the gulf oil spill has cost BP an estimated 1.6 billion USD. This figure can be itemized as follows:

- 25 million USD in grant money given to the states of Alabama, Florida, and Mississippi
- 60 million USD allocated towards the construction of barrier islands off the coast of Louisiana
- 1.4 billion USD accrued as of 18 June 2010 in cleanup efforts (tabulated at a rate of 33 million USD per day since the incident)

The above figures *do not* include costs pertaining to current and future lawsuits or the over 6700 compensation claims filed, although 1000 claims have already been settled.

Energy analysts at *Barclay Capital* project losses totaling 22.6 billion USD will be incurred by BP, including cleanup costs, worker compensation, legal fees and lost revenue. In addition, on 16 June 2010 BP announced it will slash its capital expenditure bill and suspend dividend payments until September 2011 in order to pay for the 20 billion USD claims fund imposed upon the company by the United States. Although these figures are subject to change, it is unlikely they will decrease.

The Gulf Spill Viewed in the Context of Similar Accidents

In order to provide more insight to what these numbers truly represent, it is helpful to view them in perspective to comparable incidents. For example, the *Exxon Valdez* disaster of 1989 caused 10.8 million gallons of oil to be released into the Prince William Sound, a figure which when compared to the current Gulf situation, seems relatively minor. However, the *Exxon Valdez* accident shares many traits with the BP spill. The image of Exxon was irrevocably tarnished and there was a stigma attached to the brand that is still present today.

The company was highly criticized by the government and media for lack of a quick response time and refusal to acknowledge the extent of the problem. This led the public to infer they were not taking the accident seriously. The company paid 2.5 billion USD towards cleanup efforts, 1.1 billion USD in settlement costs and a 5 billion USD fine which was later successfully appealed. It is worthy to note that whereas the *Exxon Valdez* spill was limited in capacity to the vessel in which it was contained, the *Deepwater Horizon* well, for obvious reasons, is not.

Although not accidental, the Gulf War oil spill of 1991 is still considered the greatest in terms of ecological damage and oil loss. It is estimated 450 to 520 million gallons were released into the Persian Gulf, and its effects on the region's ecosystem are still felt today.

It is possible the BP Oil spill will reach that magnitude according to an analysis by Stephen Wereley, associate professor of mechanical engineering at *Purdue University*. His findings indicate an astounding 56,000 to 84,000 barrels are being released daily. This analysis was performed using a technique known as particle image velocimetry, which tracks particles and the velocity at which they travel. The aforementioned figure includes smaller amounts of methane, but it could still bring the total amount of the oil spill into the 500 to 600 million gallon range if BP can have relief wells in place by mid-August 2010.

Consumer Impact of the Crisis

Domestically the damage regarding gas prices have been minimized, and they are congruent with market averages. But BP and its response to the accident have already diminished consumer confidence in the brand. In addition to the social impact imposed upon Gulf area businesses, individuals will be affected on an even broader scale. The seafood industry is demonstrably damaged, and has subsequently raised its prices. BP shareholders have been significantly affected financially, with a 20 percent drop in stock value since the incident and the suspension of dividend payments.

A lesser publicized implication is the U.S. government imposed 6 month moratorium on off shore drilling operations, which is having a profound effect on many. This moratorium will force the United States to rely more heavily on foreign oil, and will defer 19 percent of deepwater oil production until 2015 to 2016. To put it differently, the loss in oil production over this six month period will not be recouped for five to six years, in which time oil from Middle Eastern sources will have to be acquired to satisfy demand. Also, the suspension in off shore drilling will result in 165 to 330 million USD in lost wages and could cost 20,000 oil related jobs by the end of the year. This includes all enterprises related to production, processing, and transport of oil.

The severity of this disaster is evidenced on many levels, but the potential financial damage and subsequent consumer impact is realized in the projected costs that are to be incurred from it.

From *Economic Times*, June 18, 2010. Copyright © 2010 by Jkalal Assar. Reprinted by permission of Jkalal Assar.